THE END OF TIME

JOSEF PIEPER

THE END OF TIME

A Meditation on the Philosophy of History

translated by

MICHAEL BULLOCK

PANTHEON BOOKS INC
NEW YORK

Original German Title:
ÜBER DAS ENDE DER ZEIT

Library of Congress Catalog Card No. 54-9501

Printed in U.S.A.

To

ANNE BIERMANN

and

CLEMENS MÜNSTER

friends from the beginning

CONTENTS

9

CHAPTER III

CONCLUSION

Who can hope to obtain proper concepts of the present, without knowing the future?

JOHANN GEORG HAMANN

The will, which is today growing even greater, to create a condition that shall hold within it an exemplarily complete essence of humanity and an enduring peace, is burdened by the heavy paradox that it is not humanity which is the goal of the Incarnation.

KONRAD WEISS

11

CHAPTER I

[1]

In history, it is not the past, not 'what actually happened', which is of philosophical interest. This is not what the man engaged in philosophizing wants to know, not even when his philosophizing relates specifically to history. Of course, the enquirer in the philosophy of history needs a knowledge of history (whose subject-matter is necessarily the past, even when it is the most recent past that we call 'the present'). The subject-matter of enquiry in the philosophy of history, however, is different in principle from that of history itself.

If, provisionally and speaking roughly, we understand by 'history' that happening which takes place through time, upon active and passive humanity and through its agency, then he who philosophizes, and this does not mean any professional specialist—most certainly not, it means any man who meditates upon the roots of things and lovingly seeks wisdom!—he who philosophizes asks whether this historical happening means anything over and above the merely factual, and what this meaning may be. He is there-

13

fore asking a question which is by no means of the past, but very much of the present, indeed of the future: the question of what the historical process is 'leading up to'. For the man who is spiritually existent, who is directed upon the whole of reality, in other words, for the man who philosophizes, this question of the *end* of history is, quite naturally, more pressing than the question of 'what actually happened'.

It is no less natural that this question (what it is leading up to), now operative on a widening front, should attain an all the more painful topicality the more historical happening itself shakes man's foundations—and so make it necessary, indeed for the first time possible, for him to ask philosophical questions. Everyone is aware of the extent to which the question of the end of history is today exercising the minds of men. This results in a multiplicity of abortive answers, which win equally premature approbation and support—all of which in conjunction leads to those particular forms of sectarian apocalyptic which must be regarded as typical 'phenomena of the age', whose pronouncements are, for the most part, beyond discussion, but which must undoubtedly be taken seriously as a symptom.

We shall, of course, do well to oppose to this kind of overheated interest in 'eschatological' questions an especially high measure of sobriety and exactitude, indeed the explicit renunciation of any answer.

The most sober rejoinder that can be given to the question as to the end of time is this: Should the question not be left alone altogether, since it is scarcely possible to answer it?

This demand presupposes that such an enquiry can simply be dropped. There is, however, a great deal to suggest that the question of the end of history cannot be suspended at all, that it will 'in any case' be asked, and indeed answered. This seems at least to be true of the Christian aeon, of the period *post Christum natum*. Aristotle was still able to hold the opinion that the process of history, like that of nature, is a cycle that continually repeats itself—so much so that, as he explicitly states,[1] even men's opinions are identically repeated, 'not once or twice, not a few times, but an infinite number of times'. It is no longer possible however, *post Christum natum*, seriously to think thus. We can 'omit' neither the concept of the beginning, of the creation out of nothingness (nor this concept of nothingness itself, which is the truly radical one), nor the concept of the end. This, it seems to me, is to be numbered amongst the changes which entered into the world of man on the basis of the event 'revelation in Christ'. To render conceivable the idea that history is *not* a directed happening, that it is *not*—however manifold its stratification—a process with a beginning and an end, it would be necessary to accomplish the task, seemingly impossible, however great the will to it, of entirely abandoning the spiritual area of that tradition which has

15

received its stamp from Christianity. Whoever says 'historical development' has already said and thought that history possesses an irreversible direction; this applies all the more to anyone who says 'progress'. In the most innocent use of the words 'already' and 'still' ('the Greeks already knew . . .', 'the ancients were still aware . . .')—such turns of phrase always contain the implication that history is leading up to something, that a particular state—of perfection or of impoverishment—is the *end-state*.

It therefore appears impossible to reflect upon history in a spirit of philosophical enquiry, without at the same time enquiring, in some sense or other, as to the End. This question cannot be 'left alone'.

[2]

But is it not unanswerable? In what manner can precise information ever be given in reply to the question of the issue of history, bearing in mind that it is to be—*philosophical* information.

This immediately raises a host of fresh questions; the interrelationship is extremely intricate.

We will begin by asking the counter-question: Can a precise answer be given to any other philosophic question—'precise' in the sense of 'characterizing and enunciating the core of the subject-matter'? Can, for example, the question: 'What, in general and in the last analysis, is cognition?'—can this question be precisely answered? At all events, the endeavours of philosophers, extending over several thousand years, have so far failed to bring forth the fruit of such an answer. And the fact that these endeavours have been 'fruitless' does not entitle us to suggest abandoning the question of the nature of cognition, nor philosophical enquiry as a whole.

Is there not a difference here, however? Can he who enquires after the nature of cognition not proceed from a basis in experience which is immediately 'available' to the enquirer? Does he not know, from experience, that there is sense-perception, sight, hearing, smell, taste, touch; that there is some sort of apprehension of non-sensuous matters, that there are self-cognition, thought, contemplation and divination? Philosophical enquiry as to the nature of cognition as a whole rests upon this, indeed refers to it. But to what experiential foundation could I refer in answering, or even in considering, the question of the outcome of history? Anyone enquiring as to the end of time in terms of the philosophy of history is, in fact, undoubtedly in a special situation. But, as will be shown, the special nature of his situation does not consist in its being different in principle from that of anyone else who philosophizes; it consists in the fact that an element inherent in all philosophizing in general appears here with greater intensity.

It happens in all vital philosophizing that the sphere of the 'purely philosophical' has perforce to be overstepped into the sphere of pronouncements whose nature it is to be, not the result of human cognitive endeavour, but brought to view prior to all intellectual activity and as something received or to be received. And it is the most authentically philosophical impulse of enquiry, directed upon the first principles and roots of things, in virtue of which the boundary between philosophy and 'theology', 'faith' or 'revelation' is overstepped—so that, accordingly, a philosophizing which insisted on remaining 'purely philosophical' would be false to itself and actually cease to be philosophical. It is a peculiarity of philosophic enquiry, inherent in the matter itself, that it stands from the outset in a fully-fledged 'contrapuntal' relationship to theology; there is no philosophical question which, if it really wants to strike the ground intended by itself and in itself, does not come upon the primeval rock of theological pronouncements. And it is this peculiarity, which falls to the lot of all philosophizing, which appears in an extremely intensified form in the case of the philosophy of history—about which we shall have more to say later.

Above all, however, it is important to recognize this association with theology as an element of all philosophizing. Let us go back to the example of the question: What is cognition, in general and in the last analysis? It is true that for the philosophical discussion and consideration of this question there is certainly an experiential basis. As I press forward with the question, however, the moment will come when I shall have to look at the correspondence, which we always find to have been there in advance, between the objective reality of being on the one hand and human cognitive power on the other; the moment will come at which we shall have to ask the question which Heidegger[2] has formulated thus: 'Whence does the assertion of representation derive the injunction to take its direction from the object and to accord with correctness?'—which means, whence does the exerciser of the cognitive faculty receive 'the direction toward the existent',[3] what constitutes the inner reason for the dependence of cognition upon being? No doubt this, in the very innermost realm of the roots of a philosophical ontology, is one of the shapes assumed in a certain moment by the question of the nature of cognition; undoubtedly, without an answer to this question no statement can be made as to what cognition is, in general and in the last analysis. But it is no less evident that this subterranean question— whence does cognition derive its dependence upon the existent?—cannot be answered otherwise than by a theological pronouncement. What happens, however, one may ask—above all when one looks at modern philosophy—what happens when he who philosophizes repudiates any association with theo-

19

logy determined in this manner? Two things may happen: Either the philosophical enquiry, which at the outset is genuine, that is to say, directed upon the roots of things, is suddenly called to a halt—for reasons, it may be, of a tidy demarcation of fields of investigation—*without* there being any cause for this inherent in the nature of the enquiry itself or in the nature of its object.[4] Or the philosophical impulse is suppressed at the very inception of the question, in that philosophy deems itself one special science alongside others and confines itself to certain specialized questions (of a formal-logical nature, for instance). Thoroughly worthy findings may be expected from a specialist philosophy of this sort—only it is not philosophy in the sense of Plato and Aristotle and the great Western tradition!

[4]

If, however, one accepts this ancient concept of philosophy as valid, then one must say: A philosophizing which refuses to be methodologically open toward theology and to reach an understanding with it, is quite simply unphilosophical. This however— we return with one resolute step to the road of our initial question—this does not merely apply to the philosophy of history 'as well'; it applies to the latter more intensely and 'above all'. There are several reasons for this 'above all'.

First: History is a process, a happening that runs through time; it 'goes its way'. Now this 'way thither' is inconceivable without a notion of whence and whither; every view of history, whether explicitly or not, is determined by some sort of conception of beginning and end; even the doctrine of eternal recurrence (that there is neither beginning nor end) is an assertion of this kind. Concerning the beginning and end of history there are, however, no human experiences; beginning and end cannot be apprehended in the concrete course of history. On this point there can be no assertions that are the result of an intellectual investigation of reality. The beginning and end of human history are conceivable only on acceptance of a pre-philosophically traditional interpretation of reality; they are either 'revealed' or they are inconceivable. If on the other hand, however, the possibility of philosophical enquiry into the nature of history depends upon the beginning and end of the historical process somehow entering the field of vision of the enquirer, and upon history becoming apprehensible as a 'going' from a beginning towards an end—then it is perfectly clear why the philosophy of history must find itself especially dependent upon the theological counterpoint anterior to it.

Second: The question of the man who philosophizes about history, that is, of the man who looks at the whole and at the roots of things, runs: What is it that really takes place there?—Now, if someone were to answer: the disintegration of a culture takes place,

21

or: the rise of a world empire occurs, or: economic development comes about; or: a class conflict is enacted—in such answers the philosophical question as to what really is and, in the last analysis, happens in history would manifestly remain unappeased. What really and in the deepest analysis happens in history is salvation and disaster. These, however, are concepts that can be apprehended only on the basis of revelation—although, on the other hand, they are certainly not concepts which the human spirit could abstain from thinking (if it were to attempt to do so, they would establish their dominion in dreams—with great justice it has been remarked that the figure really indicated in anxiety dreams is the man who has lost his salvation). He who philosophizes *cannot* ignore salvation and disaster, this core of history which is accessible only to the believer—unless he ignores that at which philosophical enquiry is aimed *per definitionem*. The historian as a specialist in a particular field of research may, perhaps, expressly restrict his field of vision to the empirically apprehensible element of historical reality. But the claim of the philosophy of history to be aimed at the whole and at the foundations can no more be sustained if the concepts salvation and disaster are excluded, than can the vitally existing, historically active and passive man 'withdraw' from this core of all happening to a 'merely' economic or political or scientific activity (for—whether we will or no, whether we see or no—it is our very own salvation or disaster that 'actually' comes to pass in history). One can, of course, refuse to see history in this light at all; in that case no further argument is possible. From the standpoint of the believer such a refusal would look like the 'astonishing' explanation of which the imprisoned Socrates speaks: 'that I am sitting here because my body is made up of bones and sinews that can be relaxed or tensed . . . and that this is the reason why I am sitting here with my knees bent', whereas in truth his own ethical decision not to flee was the cause of his imprisonment—otherwise 'these sinews and bones would long since have been in Megara or amongst the Boeotians'.[5] Similarly, one may intend to operate exclusively with psychologico-politico-sociological categories in the consideration of history. But the crux of the matter, the real core of the process, will not be attained after such a fashion.

Not that he who philosophizes could ever reach the point of being able to identify *in concreto* the character of an event in terms of salvation or disaster. We are moving here within the realm of the *mysterious*—in the strictest sense. And even for the believer, the history of salvation 'within' history is not to be apprehended concretely. Of the *dispositio mundi* (an expression which is scarcely translatable: what is meant is the guidance of world events which designs, orders and disposes from afar)—of the 'disposition of the world' Thomas says:[6] 'On this subject even the highest angels are forever receiving revelations of new things, till the Day of Judgement'. This is said

23

in protest against inordinately over-hasty 'theologians of history', who seek to propagate the belief that the 'meaning' of the concrete events taking place here and now can be grasped and demonstrated in terms of the history of salvation.—Nonetheless, it is of crucial importance that in philosophizing about history the area of possible interpretation should not be over-hurriedly closed; that it should be considered and recognized that the true and ultimate reality in the happening of history, though it cannot be apprehended in detail, is the *mysterium* of salvation and disaster.—This is a second reason why precisely in questions of the philosophy of history the adoption of ultimate positions cannot be left aside.

Third: What is really asserted in revelation is not a 'world picture', not interpretation of reality in the sense of an ontology. What is revealed is, firstly, the history of salvation; an answer is given not to the question, 'what is?', but to the question, 'what has happened?' (and, 'what is going to happen?'). It treats of a single stream of historical happening—starting with the Creation, the beginning *per se*, ending with the Judgement on the Last Day, and between beginning and end the history of the Fall of Man, the awaiting, the Logos made flesh, the agony on the cross, the Resurrection, the Ascension of the God-man.—Here again we have a reason for the particular closeness of the association of philosophy of history with theology: the enquirer in philosophy of history, when he refers back to theology, strikes the exact centre of theological pronouncement, which is a pronouncement concerning the historical process of the salvation of man. Whereas the enquiry of, say, ontological philosophy, although it too, if it penetrates deep enough, also calls for reference back to theology, does not come to grips with the essential point of theological pronouncement, but, so to speak, strikes a marginal area. An inner affinity in principle of an especial kind may, therefore, be said to exist between the philosophy and theology of history.

[5]

The special and distinctive element in the situation of the enquirer in the philosophy of history is further revealed by the following consideration. A philosophy of history which refuses to refer back to theology ceases to be philosophy and starts to become pseudo-philosophy—but in a much more radical sense than is the case with the rest of philosophy. We are not moving here within the region of 'advice', which should be 'followed' by the man who is philosophizing about history (in order, for instance, to arrive at results which, as the saying goes, are desirable 'from the Christian point of view'). No, what we are asserting here is this: Wherever reference back to theology is rejected, the philosophical character of the questions asked is destroyed *realiter*; the enquiry simply ceases to be directed upon the roots of things, and hence ceases to be of human importance outside the merely specialist field. And this is true 'above all' of the philosophy of history: in such a case it does not come into being at all, not even as a question and *in initio*!

One may always, with some justice, hold the opinion that it may be possible to cast some light upon the nature of cognition, say, even without referring back to the pre-philosophic tradition (though such philosophizing necessarily lacks that spice which is present only in the most extreme radicality of enquiry and which distinguishes the pronouncements of philosophy, as philosophical, from the pronouncements of the special sciences). All the same, there may be, in a diluted sense, a philosophical ontology that does not explicitly ask the question as to the 'I am that I am' (although it is precisely philosophical ontology which Aristotle described as 'a divine science'). In the case of the philosophy of history, however, no provisionality is possible; in so far as it declines to refer back to theology it does not descry its subject matter at all; it is altogether unable to obtain a serious view of the totality of history; from the outset it fails to live up to the claim made by its title.

This conclusion is far from being merely an abstract thesis; it receives almost uncanny confirmation from the findings of experience. Anyone who looks up 'Philosophy of History' in the several-volume *Handbook of Philosophy* which appeared in 1930 and is the most recent and systematic work of its kind (in Germany), will find that the exposition opens with the following words: 'The principal forms of the systems of the philosophy of history formulated up to the present are either of merely antiquarian interest . . .' —it can be seen that judgement is here being passed on the basis of an extremely wide-sweeping demand, not simply on the same plane as these systems 'formulated up to the present', but from a vantage-point which seems to offer a more comprehensive view; in this manner, of course, comparison with the old philosophy of history is positively invited—again: 'The principal forms of the systems of the philosophy of history formulated up to the present are either of merely antiquarian interest, or they must still be capable of rendering visible a quite definite, objectively essential side of historical reality . . . These systems will here be submitted to this test. How—it must be asked—are we to elucidate with the traditional categories such questions as . . .' Now the reader expects the naming of those problems of the philosophy of history which are regarded as crucial, such problems as 'the meaning of history as a whole', 'progress or decay'. To his astonishment, however, he finds the sentence concluded as follows: 'How are we to elucidate . . . problems such as are posed by the development . . . of the Dutch group-portrait'. The almost grotesque character of this problem is scarcely diminished by the fact that, alongside the Dutch portrait-group, which continues to be the true model, Roman law and French tragedy are also named. The important thing is that a problem of this kind most certainly cannot be deemed philosophical in the sense of Plato or Augustine or Thomas Aquinas and that, in view of the high degree of critico-historical consciousness, no such claim is made for it. For him who is philosophizing out of the Western tradition such answers, indeed such questions, must remain inadequate; they are simply 'not enough'—however 'interesting' they may appear ('interestingness' is not actually a quality of philosophical knowledge).

The publication referred to here is not an isolated phenomenon without relation to others, rather is it thoroughly representative. Thus for example, in a paper, written as a report, on *Contemporary Philosophy of History*,[7] the discussion is confined to problems which, from the viewpoint of the original concept 'philosophy', could never be regarded as philosophical.[8]

Thus the ancient chronicles, that begin with Adam and Eve and end with the Antichrist (although they lay no claim to being philosophy of history, but merely to be representing a temporally and spatially limited sector of the world process—and incidentally fitting it into a totality of meaning)—these chronicles are more philosophical in their approach than that sort of modern 'philosophy of history' in which the subject matter, the totality of history, is no longer touched upon at all. Alfred Weber has given clear expression to this fact: The philosophy of history has

ceased to exist, its place has been taken by the sociology of culture.[9] This expresses an accurate self-
understanding. What remains contestable, of course,
is the apparent implication that the place in the
structure of human existence occupied by philosophic
reflection can be filled by something else. Man
philosophizes in any case—if not in the authentic
sense, then in the sense of pseudo-philosophy; if not in
referring back to a true and legitimate pre-philosophical tradition, then in referring back to a false belief or
unbelief (unbelief is far from implying that a person
'believes' nothing!). And the question may be asked
whether a connexion does not perhaps exist between
the absence of a genuine association of enquiry in
the philosophy of history with a true theology, that is
to say, the absence of a genuine philosophy of history—
in this sense—on the one hand, and on the other the un-
restrained proliferation of Utopian-millennrian expect-
ations of intra-historical salvation, above all on the
soil of the 'social religions'.[10]

[6]

If, in the course of the discussion, I continually
refer to the pronouncements of Christian theology,
the only genuine theology to be encountered at all in
the European quarter of the globe—this is not the
result of fortuitous 'theological interests'; it is not a
matter of a 'religious outlook'. I do so because other-

wise the enquiry would lose its philosophical character and would therefore simply no longer be worth while.

Moreover such references do not of themselves mean that I am 'speaking as a theologian'. Theology is not something primary, but something secondary. The primary thing, which is presupposed by theology, is a body of traditional pronouncements which are believed to have been revealed, not to have come into being through human interpretation of reality, but, as Plato[11] puts it, to 'have come down from a divine source'. Now theology is the human endeavour to interpret this body of tradition out of itself, by ordering it and weighing it.[12] This, however, I have no intention of doing. But I presuppose both the primary thing, the tradition assumed in faith to be revealed, as well as the secondary thing, the theological interpretation of this body of tradition. I refer to the interpretation of the pronouncement of revelation set down in theological writings—which can, of course, be done in earnest only if this pronouncement anterior to theology is simultaneously accepted as valid, in other words, if it is 'believed'. Again, I am not speaking as a theologian, but referring back to the information provided by theology— and, by so doing, calling to mind something which was formerly self-evident not just to the Christian West, but equally to Plato, Virgil, and Cicero, and also to Lao-tse: that theology forms a part of general education.

Philosophizing does not become intellectually easier by referring back to theology; to be sure, reference back to a true theology in philosophizing renders the nature of reality more deeply accessible, but at the same time its mysteriousness becomes more compellingly manifest; the greater the extent to which knowledge discloses being, the more profoundly does the mystery of the existent unveil itself within it. This truth, however, which is characteristic of all philosophizing as a whole, again applies 'above all' to the philosophy of history.

A Christian philosophy of history, which derives all the evil in the world from the revealed fact of original sin, may now suppose for an instant that things have become 'more plausible' and 'simpler'. Yet to the vision that penetrates deeper this proves to be an illusion—notwithstanding the fact that this derivation, because it is true, stands infinitely higher in its power to disclose reality than all other derivations (such as from an original evil principle operating alongside God, or from a tragic contradiction within God himself). Within original sin, however, a new mystery becomes manifest, much more enigmatic and impenetrable than the empirically encounterable evil in the world. Or, the 'enlightened' philosophy of progress is intellectually just as simple as the philosophy of despair of radical pessimism, which foresees the end of history as decay, chaos, self-destruction, non-fulfilment. A philosophy of history dealing with the end, however, which refers back to the pronouncement of the Apocalypse that in the last days the Antichrist will establish a world dominion of evil, and which nevertheless will not and cannot be a philosophy of despair—of such a philosophy of history no one will expect an intellectually simple view of history. It may perhaps be said that a philosophy of history which is in this sense Christian constitutes the most intellectually arduous task that can be set in the whole domain of philosophy.

[8]

In respect of enquiry in the philosophy of history relating to the end of time there is a special reason for this—once more intensified—complication. It consists in the fact that the theological pronouncement to which this enquiry has, above all, to refer is made in the guise of *prophecy*.

On the other hand, there exists an inner co-ordination of history with prophecy. 'History', involves 'happening'; but not everything which 'happens' is 'history'. The flash of lightning, the fall of the stone, the flowing of water—all this is unhistorical happening. That a plant germinates, grows, blossoms, bears fruit and dies, or the life-cycle of an animal—this is already a little closer to the essence of history, but it is not yet truly history. Not even everything that happens to us humans is history in the full and strict sense. It happens to us that we are born, grow up, age, die—but this does not yet constitute our history; biological processes, even if their subject is man, do not amount, of themselves, to history. The history of man—this is rather the unique commingling of free decision and fate; the encounters which fall to his lot in this unrepeatable moment of life; man's 'path', in so far as it is determined by his particular response to what destiny causes to befall him (whether this is a beloved person, a teacher, an antagonist or the gain or loss of possessions, health, beauty or the innate gift of aptitudes, temperament, 'constitution'). The concepts associated with the essential nature of history are freedom, decision, uniqueness, unrepeatability, un-interchangeability, unpredictable capacity for varia-tion, the individually solitary; by these, historical happening is distinguished from the unhistorical hap-pening of nature. Because this is so, however, because history is not simply the 'unfolding' of something previously given that was not yet unfolded, because it is not simply 'development'—for this reason, in the sphere of history the concretely future cannot be calculated in advance, neither by the stars nor by statistics. But there may be *prophecy*. Prophecy is the sole form of prediction co-ordinated with the essence of history. Just as it is of the essence of history that what is to come cannot be calculated in advance in its concrete 'What', 'How', 'When', from the fund of experience (that is, from the past),

so it is part of the concept of prophecy to be a prediction that does not require any foothold in experience. This is not the full concept of prophecy, of
which something like this also forms a part: It is not
some indifferent aspect of the future which is foretold, but an event related to the inmost kernel of
history, to the realization of salvation and disaster;
it is one of the conceptual elements of prophecy that
it has its place in the history of salvation.

In the sphere of history there is, of course, prognosis. But it is essential to the concept of prognosis
that it stands on 'footholds' in the present; indeed,
the art of prognosis consists in discovering in the fund
of experience itself pointers to the future, which is
concealed in the present. This distinguishes prognosis from prophecy; as does also the other fact, that
prognosis necessarily proceeds towards the probable.
—And statistics? Can it not be predicted with con-
siderable exactitude how many suicides, divorces,
accidents there will be in a particular city over a particular period of time? Here we must speak in completely concrete terms: It could, of course, have been
stated in the summer of 1944, on the basis of statistics,
how many fatal traffic accidents there would be in the
city of Danzig in July 1945—provided that the city
of Danzig existed and that there was still 'traffic'
there at all. That this condition would not hold good,
however—this could *not* be predicted on the basis of
statistics. This is also the point at which to recall
Pascal's aphorism:[13] 'Could anyone enjoying the

34

friendship of the King of England, the King of Poland and the Queen of Sweden have believed that he might be without refuge and without asylum in the whole world?'—a sentence written in the year 1656, the year of the deposition of the King of Poland, two years after the abdication of the Queen of Sweden and seven years after the execution of the King of England. The truly historical event, concrete in every respect (when?, where?, who?), cannot be foreseen at all in prognostication.

The claim of prophecy, however, is aimed at precisely this. The Messianic prophecies of the Old Testament, which remain the model of all prophecy, foretell the passion of the Servant of God—an occurrence which could not have been predicted by any sort of calculation, a fact for which no expectation could be found in the contents of history available to experience, an event in the highest sense historical, grounded on an unconstrained and absolutely free 'Yea'. Because prophecy relates to that which is in the strictest sense historical, it is therefore of its essence that it brings to view not a result arising out of the interpretive penetration of what can be experienced, but something made known by revelation, a 'vision', the announcement of something pertaining to the indeterminate future.

But why is the situation of the man enquiring after the end of time in terms of the philosophy of history complicated by the fact that the theological pronouncement associated with his enquiry is made in the guise of prophecy? The answer must lead to the discussion of a number of problems.

First: Prophecy which is not yet 'fulfilled', that is, prophecy which is still prediction, still 'unconfirmed', is for the natural man altogether the most 'scandalous' form in which a revealed announcement can confront him ('scandalous' in the New Testament sense).[14] To be sure, the fact of revelation, which means an announcement that comes to us 'from without' with a claim to absolute truth, at which human cognitive power could never have arrived of itself—this fact alone is not easily accepted by the subject who is awakened to critical consciousness, that is to say, by 'modern man'. All the same, an already 'concluded' revelation, which has been fashioned into the accepted property of tradition by centuries of theological interpretation and has thereby become, so to speak, historically legitimized, seems to be something less scandalous and aggressive—something so little aggressive that it becomes positively needful to 'render oneself synchronous' to the fact of the revelation again (as Kierkegaard has put it) by an explicit, almost violent act of reflection and so call to mind the scandalous character of the revelation, its incommensurability with the spheres both of nature and of culture. In the case of a still 'unconfirmed' prophecy this is not even necessary—provided that its claim to being revelation is taken seriously! A prophecy whose absolute claim is accepted, a prophecy relating to our own future that has not yet happened (that which is truly ours is the future—the future tense is the tense of the existential, whereas the past is of existential consequence only in so far as the future is rooted in it)—a prophecy relating to our own future is *ipso facto* and in every case a challenge and a 'scandal'.—'How differently the Apocalypse affects us from the predictions of Isaiah!'—it is John Henry Newman[15] who ponders this question: and he simultaneously proposes to explain the attitude of the Jews at the turn of the ages towards the Messianic prophecies 'by our own, at present, towards the Apocalypse'. But this leads to a new idea, which will be considered explicitly later on. Suffice it for now that it has become clear that the scandalousness, the incommensurable element in revelation as a whole, is naturally most sharply defined in the prophecy which refers to the future of the people living at any given time. On the other hand, there may be some connexion between this scandalousness and the power of attraction peculiar to the profoundly unhistorical, and hence in principle inadequate, forms of prediction, such as astrology.

It is of the essence of prophecy that it can be understood only to the extent to which it is being fulfilled—

and even then only by the believer. It is hardly necessary to say how greatly this fact also complicates, distinctively, enquiry in the philosophy of history about the end of time. The attitude of the Jews to the Messianic prophecies, of which Newman speaks, is something very remarkable: They did not recognize or accept the fulfilment of the prophecies, *although* they believed, that is to say, although they accepted the claim of the prophecies to be Divine Revelation. And here we seem to have something paradigmatic, something typical of the understanding of prophecies in general.

If an historically educated Roman on the staff of Pontius Pilate, well acquainted with the scriptures of this singular and, from a religious-historical point of view, very interesting people, the Jews, and familiar with all these prophecies, but obviously not accepting them as being in any way the word of God—if this Roman, despite his wide knowledge, had failed to perceive the fulfilment of the prophecies taking place before his eyes, this would have been entirely natural. This would have been just as natural as that a radically secularized mankind, with an élite committed to a rationalistic theory of society, will be utterly incapable of recognizing the fulfilment of the Apocalyptic prophecy—since the latter will not be believingly accepted—but, on the contrary, will rather interpret the events as the realization of a stupendous advance on the part of mankind—that this will be so is itself a part of the Apocalyptic prophecy! All this is natural and nothing else could be expected; this is, so to speak, 'foreseen'. But that—as the case of the Jews shows—the believer may himself also mistake the meaning of the prophecy, if—well, if what? The problem has many levels.

It is true that prophecy, like all revelation, can be intentionally rejected. And since the predictive meaning of prophecy is only unveiled little by little, explicit, intentional approbation is invited and becomes possible only in the same measure, little by little, approbation as well as non-approbation, the Yea as well as the Nay—so that once-and-for-all approbation would be neither possible nor sufficient, by virtue of the very nature of the matter. The 'great apostasy' resulting from the events of the Apocalypse itself, and, what is more, as the theological interpretation states, the apostasy of *believers*, which is explicitly foretold, is accordingly contained as a possibility in principle in the essence of the prophecy.

That prophecy only becomes intelligible in the measure of its fulfilment, 'when events are preparing themselves and their elements are already beginning to be historically present':[16] this is—further—so true that, as again John Henry Newman[17] has said, only 'the event is the true key to prophecy'; the predictive meaning of a prophecy becomes totally clear only to the man who looks back upon it from the vantage point of its historical fulfilment. The questionable nature of the proposal to make some valid pronouncement concerning the end of time thus appears even more obscure. Furthermore, this proposition is also applicable on a lower plane. If, for instance, that enigmatic character Nostradamus (whose significance is not under discussion here— we will merely say that in this field there are many things which can be illumined only with difficulty or not at all, and that even magic in the demonic sense cannot be excluded in principle)—if then Nostradamus should have foretold modern bombing-planes together with the underground air-raid shelters associated with them, by the same token no one could have deciphered these predictions *prior* to their realization, and, so to speak, profited by them (which, by the way, men were unable to do afterwards either!).

The 'difficulty' in relation to a prophecy is therefore highly multiform; it lies in the sphere of cognition as well as of volition. We will leave this latter on one side; we are speaking of the situation of the man conducting an enquiry in the philosophy of history, where it is cognition that is involved,

The complexity of the situation for the knower, and also for the believer, looked at more closely, resides in the fact that theological interpretation of the prophecy concerning the end of history, to which interpretation the enquirer in the philosophy of history is compelled to refer back, is in turn dependent upon the apprehension and interpretative penetration of historical phenomena themselves. 'A progressive possibility of theological interpretation of the Apocalypse'[18] does not, therefore, exist otherwise than in the degree to which the historical process itself is accomplished and intellectually elucidated.

We have already stated that if we are enquiring into the essential nature of history, the conjunction of philosophy and theology applies more fully than elsewhere; here it emerges that this more complete conjunction is valid *for theology as well*. If it is already true of the theological act as a whole that it is bound to the presupposition of a genuinely philosophical attitude and education, this has even more unconditional validity the moment theological interpretation relates to the Apocalyptic prophecy of the end of history. And one may venture the assertion that just as the philosophy of history has fallen into decay because it has refused to accept the information afforded by theology, so the cause of the infertility, indeed insignificance, of the average contemporary commentary on the Apocalypse is to be sought in, amongst other things, the lack of philosophic earnestness behind the enquiry; at all events, wherever a vital and humanly important theological interpretation of the Apocalypse is to be found (for instance, in the work of Erik Peterson, Ethelbert Stauffer or Philipp Dessauer), there simultaneously appears an unmistakable preoccupation with the philosophy of history fired by immediate participation in the experience of the age, and manifested through the most profound inward concern at what is happening in the world to-day, 'really and fundamentally'. It may very well be thought, therefore, that the decay of the philosophy

41

of history is in no small measure to be blamed upon theology (not 'Christianity', not 'the Church', but 'theology', that is, upon human intellectual endeavour to interpret the material of revelation).

[10]

Should one then summarize by saying: Philosophy presupposes theology, but also conversely theology presupposes philosophy, and this relationship of mutual reflexive determination applies 'above all' to enquiry into the essential nature of history? That would be far too imprecise. There cannot be a reflexive determination in both directions in the same sense; philosophy cannot presuppose theology in the same sense as theological interpretation presupposes philosophy. Let us try to illuminate this complex interfusion so that its structure stands out clearly.

Amongst the innumerable hardly credible 'true stories' of recent years, is that of the two mysterious figures who were found among German soldiers in a prisoner of war camp in the U.S.A. No one understood their language; no one knew where they had come from or the name or the homeland of their people. Chance interrogation by a specialist, who was acquainted with the languages of several Asiatic peoples, elicited that these two men were Tibetans. These young men, wanting to earn money, had crossed the northern frontier of their country into

Soviet Russian territory, for one summer, as they thought. This, however, was the summer of the year 1941. The two found themselves suddenly thrust into uniform, given a hurried training, armed with rifles and sent to the front. They were taken prisoner by the Germans. After some time they were drafted into the auxiliary services of the German army in France, and then, after the invasion, once more armed with rifles and 'thrown in' on the Normandy front. They were taken prisoner again, along with thousands of German troops, voyaged for days westward across a vast expanse of water, and ended in this camp. After they had told their story they asked the only man who understood them one more question, which was obviously worrying them greatly: what this shooting was really all about. It may, therefore, confidently be assumed that these two Tibetans did not understand anything whatsoever of what was happening in the world—nothing of the structure of a modern State, nothing of the constellation of the powers, nothing of the intermingling of political, economic and technical power, nothing of the integration of all powers into a few world-spanning empires; indeed, the world as a whole, the earth as a planet, was undoubtedly not present to them at all. At the same time, however—as is always the case with people who do not belong to the sphere of world-European civilization—at the same time it is permissible to conjecture that the two Tibetans were pious men, which does not mean that they led exemplary lives, but that they were well instructed in the sacred traditions of their priest-ruled people and convinced that all that happens is in the hands of the gods, that not only the destiny of the individual, but also the whole course of the world is guided by divine powers. On the pre-assumption of a faith in the meaning of historical happening as a whole, nourished by sacred tradition, these two Tibetans, although uprooted from the soil of their natural existence, nevertheless possessed an inward sense of their own position and direction within this happening, impenetrably enigmatic as it must have seemed to them *in concreto*. This is as indubitable as that the most extensive knowledge of concrete history, the most brilliant cultural-sociological analysis of Roman law, of the Dutch group portrait, or even of the contemporary constellation of world politics, *without* this conviction of an, in some way, absolutely guaranteed meaning of history as a whole, is *not* capable of affording this inner sense of position and direction. This comparison does not concern pious generalities. Rather can the superiority of the man who believes (even if he does not know) over the unbeliever (even if he knows) be very precisely indentified, for instance in those extreme situations which history again and again holds ready for man: a superiority expressed as inner inviolability, as the capacity, above all, not to despair.

Now the real reason for recalling the strange story of the two Tibetans is this: it exhibits, as though artificially isolated and distilled, a *purely believing* relation to history, an opinion and pre-conception which, although the concrete material of experience escapes it, is nonetheless most certainly directed upon that which *really* happens. Such a relation to history, consisting of naked faith, may not, in less pure realizations, be of such rare occurrence at all. Of course, it is differentiated not only from the relation to history of the historian and the cultural sociologist, but no less from that of the enquirer in the philosophy of history, as well as from that of the theologian (after all, theology is not mere credulity, but scientifically reflected interpretation of that which is believed, carried out in accordance with a philosophic approach). But the presupposition of both the philosophy and the theology of history is faith, that is, receptive acceptance of the revealed word concerning history. And only on the basis of this presupposition, which is common to both the man who philosophizes and the theologian, is there 'enacted' the reciprocal relationship of philosophy and theology (which we are endeavouring to grasp more precisely): on the one hand, the pronouncements of revelation, which are accepted in faith, become increasingly 'assimilable' for philosophic thought only at the rate of theological interpretation, while, on the other hand, this theological interpretation can grow not only clearer and more exact in form, but also richer in content, at the rate at which it incorporates philosophic thought—in so far, for example, in the theological interpretation of the Apocalypse, as the contentual meaning of that which is believed to have been revealed, first becomes applicable at all, or else more applicable than was previously evident, *on the basis* of philosophical penetration of the experiential material in which this prophecy is to find its realization, as it occurs. (In this process, reference may be made to the findings of a secularized science and cultural sociology; the real kernel of the pronouncements contained in these findings may then be better understood from the vantage point of faith than by these sciences themselves.) How then, let us ask once more, is this complex relationship of reciprocal, reflexive determination between the philosophy and the theology of history to be construed? From the vantage point of the depositum of revelation, which, however, has received only the minimum of interpretation and reflective consideration, the enquirer in the philosophy of history gazes into the multiplicity of concrete happening, perceiving-examining-interpreting; this in turn makes possible a higher-calibre theological interpretation of this believed revealed word of the Apocalypse; from the vantage point of such a formally more exact, contentually more profound theological interpretation, more comprehensive, more penetrating philosophical insight into history becomes possible in turn—and so on. Do we not therefore remain, even if the serpent does form a closed ring, aware of what and where the head is?

11

Let us now cast our minds back, from the point we have reached in our discussion, to the reflection formulated at the very beginning: whether the question as to the end of time, since it is, after all, unanswerable, should not be abandoned. In part the reply to the objection has already been given; one *must* ask this question; man is incapable of leaving it unasked. But is there an answer, a *philosophical* answer? In putting this question we recollect that he who philosophizes looks primarily at things, at the being of the world which he can experience and which takes place day by day, and is not, like the theologian, looking at a body of pronouncements which he believes to be revealed. Is it, then, possible for us to find something open to experience in the historical reality before our eyes, which has some connexion with the end of time? It is self-evident that this question will have to be answered negatively for a purely immanent cultural sociology, which refuses in principle to refer back to a pre-philosophical tradition. Whoever does not recognize, after some fashion or other, a revealed pronouncement concerning the End, that man is also incapable of undergoing, in concrete historical reality, any experiences that are related to the End; he cannot even look methodically at the reality confronting him, with this in view. That is to say, he cannot even enquire about the End (in this respect secularized philosophy of history is thoroughly consistent). But is he who believingly accepts the Apocalyptic prophecy of the end of time able to experience more, to see more in concrete historical reality? I believe that this question must, in fact, be answered in the affirmative. Whoever accepts in faith the revealed prophecy of the end of history (and, it must be added, assimilates the theological interpretation of this revealed prophecy), is able to see more and, in addition, to see it *in* historical events and formations; he is able to perceive something about the events and formations which has an inner connexion with the end of time. Hearing in faith of an End to be expected in a certain shape, and instructed by the theological interpretation of what we have heard, we look at the concrete phenomena of history—and we are able to see something in them and about them which, without this, we should not see: does this proposition really hold good? Can it be stated more precisely *what* it is that we are supposed to be capable of perceiving? And what would then be *the nature* of this seeing, perceiving, experiencing?

History is always *inwardly* directed towards its end. This, of course, is inseparable from the revealed prophecy of the End: that it will happen not (or not exclusively) as a cosmic catastrophe, as the destruction of the star Earth, but as an event historical in itself, engendered by the historical process itself, in the accomplishment of history itself. If the End were exclusively a fact of the world of heavenly bodies, it could have no specific connexion with history. It would be inadmissible to say that history is inwardly directed towards the End. The object of the prophecy of the End is, however, explicitly and formally an historical event, or rather a series of historical events. And theology has, since time immemorial, understood certain historical phenomena, such as persecutions and the figure of the tyrant, to be prefigurations and preliminary forms of the end-state.

What is it, in relation to the end of time, that becomes available to the experience of the believer in the occurrences and structures of historical reality? It is this arrow pointing towards the End, it is this character of being-directed-towards-the-End, which becomes discernible in and about that which concretely happens, to the eye of him who has accepted the Apocalypse as revelation and bends his gaze upon concrete history from that vantage point.

There are many kinds of experience. In one manner I experience that iron is heavier than aluminium; in another manner I experience, independently of 'proofs' and explicit confirmations, that I am loved or hated; in yet another manner the atmosphere of poetry, the specifically poetic element in a poem, is apprehensible to me—but in each case it is undoubtedly a matter of real experience; that is to say, the differing weight of metals, the attitude of friend or foe, the inner meaning of a poem do not become evident to me through a communication from outside, but through the fact that in direct contact the things give information concerning themselves.

Further, there are experiences which can be repeated and so tested by others; and there are experiences which are not communicable in this sense. For example, the experiences of the believer are altogether incommunicable to the unbeliever. It is of the essence of faith that a complete identification takes place between the believer and the thing believed, so that the assumption that the thing believed is not true cannot even be made *in abstracto* and hypothetically. For the same reason, it is equally impossible for the unbeliever to assume, abstractly and, so to speak, 'purely theoretically', that the thing believed is true ('let us assume the Christians to be right, and let us see where this leads us'). Faith is not like a lookout tower or a telescope that can be used by everyone in a spirit of experiment. Only he who believes, with complete existential earnestness, is also able to perceive the light which falls from the believed truth upon reality.

Further, there are experiences which can be at once clearly recognized and named as to their *What* by the person who undergoes them; and there are such as cannot be expressed at once, but to begin with remain, as it were, latent. There may be experiences which reveal themselves as experiences only when something special happens. For example, I could never have predicted how the persons most closely surrounding me in my daily life would behave in an unusual, extreme situation; but now that I am living through it, I am not surprised. Without knowing it,

I expected it to be as it is—because something of these persons' inmost individuality, which only now reveals itself as having been perceived with certainty, as having been experienced, had already become perceptible to me beforehand.

Of what kind then is that experience, in virtue of which the believer perceives in concrete historical phenomena the character of being-directed-towards-the-end, their odour and flavour of the end of time as it were? It is certainly not to be numbered amongst the types of experience that can be easily repeated by anyone. Perhaps—I do not dare to speak here with entire certitude; it seems to me to be saying a great deal already to remark that in this field even the most imperceptible form of experience, which is 'only just real' means that there may be legitimate pronouncements of a philosophical nature concerning the end of time, that is to say, pronouncements made with one's eyes on *de facto* history—perhaps this seeing and experiencing is of the kind that leads first to latent knowledge, that reveals itself as really having been experienced only on the occasion of a particular historical realization, in the shape of absence of surprise. Thus for instance, the totalitarian work State, seen from the viewpoint of liberal thought, may appear something monstrously surprising in twentieth-century Europe, something unbelievably extreme— whereas the observer who regards history from the viewpoint of the Apocalypse 'recognizes' the totalitarian State, without surprise and with accurate understanding of its innermost historical tendencies and structures, as a milder preliminary form of the State of Antichrist. There is a well-tried rule of thumb, in the practical knowledge of human nature, which states that we should visualize the peculiarities of the man of whom we are seeking to form an opinion, so to speak, 'extended' into the associated morbid form (mental illnesses are, after all, in a certain sense 'exaggerations' of normal structures), and that we should then, from the vantage point of this extreme mode, take a fresh look at the normal form and learn to understand it more profoundly in itself, in its concealed, but real, meaning. Something similar may happen if we observe historical events and formations from the vantage point of the End: they become, in themselves, more profoundly apprehensible and understandable, if they are conceived *sub specie* of their, in the positive as well as in the negative, extreme configurations, in which 'normal history' presents itself to us in the visions of revealed mysteries. May it not be conceivable that, from Apocalyptic prophecy, a whole fund of such potential experiences has entered into the storehouse of the believer's *anamnesis*, which are then, at the sight of historical phenomena, and to that extent entirely *as* experiences, realized and read out from the kernel of historical reality?

12

It is of course crucial that the gaze be really directed upon concretely occurring reality and not formally upon the pronouncement of revelation, in other words, that it is really a matter of philosophy and not of theology. But is it in fact an *intelligere* that takes place here, and not rather a *credere*? What is the structure of the act performed here? I look upon things —but this reality spread out before my eyes is illuminated by a light at which I do *not* look, which is, rather, situated behind my back, but which illuminates things to my eyes only if I 'believe'.

For example, I experience things as being knowable, penetrable, accessible to the human cognitive faculty. This fact, however, that things can be 'entered upon' in cognition and by the person exercising cognition (a fact which is undoubtedly given in things themselves!)—this fact becomes really apprehensible in its core only when it enters the beam of light of the revealed word, namely, that of the Logos, in whom all things have their source. This word states that the inner manifestness, accessibility, lucidity of things has flowed into them out of the creative knowledge of the Divine Logos, simultaneously with their being, indeed as their being itself; and that it is this lucidity, stemming from the Logos, through which things become perceptible to human cognition; and that in this sense, according to the magnificently simple formulation of Thomas Aquinas, 'the reality of things themselves is their light'.[19] Undoubtedly, therefore, when I reflect upon this structure of things, their knowability, their 'truth',[20] their luminosity, I am looking the things themselves in the face; the direction of my gaze is towards the reality before my eyes; but it is equally certain that I should not descry this inmost disposition of existent things, if they did not lie in the light of the Logos, by which everything was made in the beginning, which shines down as it were from behind my back, over my shoulder. Hence what is involved here is certainly an *intelligere*, a perception in the encounter with things—but it is an *intelligere* grounded on a *credere*.

This structure, however, which finds expression in the old proposition *credo ut intelligam*, is profoundly characteristic of Western philosophizing as a whole—not only of Christian philosophizing and also not only of the philosophizing of Plato. The founder and initiator of scientific philosophizing in the narrower sense, Aristotle, likewise realizes this structure in his ontology. The most exciting conclusion of the incomparable book on Aristotle by Werner Jaeger is that, as is shown by the history of Aristotle's development, 'even behind his metaphysics there already stands the *credo ut intelligam*'.[21] The fund of truth contained in Western philosophy is largely a fund of 'insights' gained by an *intelligere* grounded on a *credere*. After this *credere* had commenced to wither away, however, it was possible at first for men to continue their acceptance of these 'insights', even without the perennial re-laying of the foundation of the *credere*. It seemed for centuries as though these were 'purely' philosophical cognitions. For a long time, however, this seeming has been recognized as illusory, and where it was impossible to derive these supposedly 'purely' philosophical insights from a co-ordinate source in a new faith, there remained and remains hardly any other course than, with progressive critical consciousness in philosophizing, to eliminate from the body of philosophical concepts such insights as have come into being on the basis of a *credere* that is no longer implemented. Thus, for instance, Kant observed the atrophy, the incipient withering away, of those propositions (as to the truth and goodness of all that is), upon which the whole of Western ontology rests. In the second edition of the *Critique of Pure Reason* he devoted to this observation a special paragraph, in which he states, with a kind of elegiac respect: These propositions have 'in modern times been erected in metaphysics almost solely *honoris causa*'. He emphasizes the extent to which 'an idea which has persisted for so long . . . must always merit an investigation of its origin—' yet Kant can do no more than find these ancient propositions 'empty', 'sterile' and 'tautological', expressly deny the assertions made in them, and in this way 'depreciate for ever' the fundamental concepts of the old ontology (as it has been said, with complete agreement, by a modern historian of philosophy).[22]

The more this process of purification advances and

55

is deemed inescapable, the more, quite naturally, must the respectful presentiment of the grandeur of these fundamental propositions, which was still felt by Kant, vanish away. And there is no question but that all insights which come about in accordance with the structure *credo ut intelligam* will fall victim to this process of purification and liquidation. This might, however, very well be every one of the basic concepts and basic propositions of the traditional philosophy of the West. And it has become almost idle to ask whether the pseudo-philosophy of the totalitarian State, that has degenerated into a mere political ideology with a utilitarian purpose, is perhaps not solely the outcome of external coercion, but to an equal extent the true result of philosophy's own inner development itself. And the man who meditates in terms of the philosophy of history upon the end of philosophy, in the wisdom of the ancients and from the vantage point of a *credere*, is horrified by the realization that in this prospective waste and desolation of the authentic province of philosophy, an inner connexion with the end-state of history described in the Apocalyptic visions may perhaps also be discernible. These visions do *not* speak of philosophy, of 'universal wisdom'—but they *do* speak of faith, of the Church, and also of political power, of 'economy', of 'propaganda'. Is it possible that this silence contains a reference to the end of philosophy? Might not —through the extinction, or rather the disregarding and shutting out, of the refulgent light of the revealed

word that shines behind the back of him who philosophizes—the whole domain 'roots of things' fall so
wholly into darkness for natural, philosophizing
Reason that it would remain enterable *only* to the
believer, accessible solely through faith in the Divine
Logos, in which indeed the primordial images of all
things dwell—and that besides this there will no
longer be any genuine philosophy at all, but only a
pseudo-philosophy, to which the domain 'roots of
things' is so completely closed that it will no longer
even enquire about it?

CHAPTER II

[1]

However the end of time is to be thought of, 'end' cannot be understood in an absolute sense.

What is meant by 'end in the absolute sense'? We always think of the concept of the end in correspondence to that of the beginning. The end is the revocation of the beginning; beginning is the Yea, end the Nay to match. End in the absolute sense would mean that the beginning in the absolute sense, that the Creation, was revoked and terminated; it would mean that just as in the *creatio* there was a production (a leading forth) out of nothingness into being, so at the end there would be a reduction (a leading back) out of being into nothingness.

It is characteristic of contemporary nihilism (whose radicality first became possible on the basis of the theological concept of the *creatio*, which was in any case not thought of in antique philosophy, and which alone rendered the concept of 'nothingness' thinkable in its extreme form)—it characterizes this nihilism, which has worked its way deep into the consciousness of the age, that it is assumed that there can be (or there should be) an end of history in this absolute sense, or even that every end, including that of the individual human being, is (or should be) a reduction into nothingness.

The wish-image of a reduction into nothingness, of an 'an-*nihil*-ation' in the most extreme sense was, within the area of the Western tradition, probably first formulated by Nietzsche. For him nihilism is not just an intellectual position, not merely the theoretical 'conviction of the absolute inability of existence to endure',[1] 'not only the result of contemplating the "in vain", and not only the belief that everything is worthy to go to destruction'.[2] Nietzsche speaks explicitly of 'destruction by the hand', seeing it, therefore, according to the pattern of a human operation, or at least of human wishing, or longing. From that point (or in the train of the same impulse which induced Nietzsche to speak in these terms) the notion of an end in the absolute sense, as something possible or even desirable, has penetrated the collective consciousness of the modern world, which in this respect is more nihilistic than might be supposed. It has even reached deep into Christendom's feeling for life.

And, moreover, the traditional theological doctrine of *annihilatio* in some degree concurs with nihilism in opposition to an idealistic doctrine of man. Firstly, *omnis creatura vertibilis est in nihil*,[3] every creature is, of itself, capable of being brought back into nothingness; more accurately speaking, the creature is, of itself, incapable of persisting in being. Secondly,

Thomas Aquinas once asked himself the question whether God could reduce the creature into nothingness. To the counter-reflection that God could not do something evil Thomas replied, 'Just as it was not a *malum* before the creation of things (that things were not), so it would also not be a *malum* if God brought back everything into nothingness';[4] 'annihilation', in so far, of course, as it was wrought by God, would be no evil. Thirdly, there is something in the world which sets the idea close to us that it would be just and right to put an end to creation—namely, sin; the world has been thrown into such disorder by man that *annihilatio* might appear an act of justice.[5] This then is the grain of truth which is also contained in nihilism.

[2]

But how is an *annihilatio*, the reduction into nothingness, to be conceived? The expression reduction, 'leading back', seems to state the senseless proposition that being and nothingness are two areas or conditions of equal reality, between which, thither and thence, there is a 'road' along which things could be led from nothingness into being and back from being into nothingness. And wherever 'annihilation' means not reduction into nothingness, not putting an end to creation, but, say, the reduction of that which has been given shape into a state of shapelessness, the transformation of cities into heaps of rubble (which, after all, are by no means 'nothing')—wherever then, it is an unauthentic annihilation that is meant, an act, a doing, a positive intervention is indeed required to bring it about. Of *annihilatio*, annihilation in the radical sense, this is not true. First we must add that he alone can annihilate who can create; *sicut solus Deus potest creare, ita solus Deus potest creaturas in nihilum redigere*,[6] just as God alone is able to create, so also is God alone able to reduce that which has been created into nothingness. This reduction into nothingness, however, would *not* be a doing, would *not* be a positive act: 'If God were to reduce something real into nothingness, this would not take place through an operation, but through his ceasing to operate'.[7] That is to say, because the creature, we ourselves and everything that is in the world, exists and 'is' solely in virtue of the uninterrupted divine act of *creatio* (what is termed 'maintenance in being' is, projected into Time, creation itself), there is no need for 'something' to happen for the creature to sink back into the nothingness from which it springs; literally 'nothing' needs to happen for this sinking back to come about, all that is required is for creation to cease happening! It is a truly uncanny thought that to dispatch the whole splendour of existing things into non-existence no 'arrangement' is needed at all; so closely does the innermost centre of our being border upon nothingness that there is no 'distance' whatsoever to be overcome. Hence there is no need whatever for an 'Apocalyptic downfall' to put an

61

end to creation and annihilate the created world. *This, however, is not the meaning of the end of history either!*

Absolute loquendo, speaking in the abstract, 'God may withdraw his operation from the things to be maintained in being: thereby they would all fall into nothingness. But "God has created all things that they might be", not that they might crumble into nothingness'.[8] This sentence quoted by Thomas, from the *Book of Wisdom* (1, 14), justifies a boldness of affirmation bordering on the monstrous: there will be no *annihilatio* at all, no End in the absolute sense! 'The being of the creature cannot come wholly to an end; the creature cannot be termed, *simpliciter,* transient at all';[9] 'even if it is transient—the creature will never fall back into nothingness';[10] 'all the works of God will remain to eternity (either in themselves, or in their causes)'.[11] The concept 'an-*nihil*-ation', 'absolute end', can have a place only in unreal thinking.

[*3*]

On the other hand, this same fact first lends full earnestness to real thinking concerning the End and gives it, so to speak, its courage.

'Heroic nihilism', which makes ready for annihilation or even supposes itself able, by the power of man himself, to bring about total extinction, real reduction into nothingness, is an attempt to withdraw into a fallacious God-likeness, into the same God-likeness which is claimed in the idealistic tendency to regard the human person as an absolute (which nihilism intends to *oppose*).

Nihilism rests on the pre-assumption that the creature possesses 'the capacity for non-existence', that it has its own origin out of nothingness in its power like something of which it can dispose, so that it could also put an end to this origin. *Potentia ad non-esse*, however, is in no wise possessed by the creature. 'If it be said that what springs from nothingness strives, of itself, toward nothingness, so that the power of not-being dwells in all created things, this is manifestly not logically correct. For all that can be said is that beings created by God strive toward nothingness *in the same manner* in which they also originated out of nothingness. But this took place solely through the power of an agent. Hence, then, the power of nothingness does not dwell in created entities; but the power to give them being or to cause the flow of being toward them to dry up dwells *in God*'—these are sentences from the *Summa contra Gentes* of Thomas Aquinas.[12] What do they say?

On the one hand they say that because the creature is a creature, that is, because it springs from nothingness, therefore it is so very powerless that it cannot even destroy, annihilate, itself. On the other hand they say that because the creature is a creature, that is, has proceeded out of that which is in the highest fashion existent, therefore it is so very existent that, if it could be destroyed at all, it could be destroyed only by the Creator himself—who, however, has created it 'that it might be'.

Hence, however immense the advances made by the technological intelligence in the perfection of the machinery of destruction, however great the increase in 'destructive efficiency' (who can have invented this technical expression of military science, 'destructive efficiency'?); however much, on the other hand, the despair of the humanity that lives on this violated earth may yearn for *annihilatio* as a deliverance—it is not given to man 'to make an end' in this absolute sense. Rather will man—in the knowledge and acknowledgement of his own creatureliness, which does not suffice either to produce being or to abolish it—have to make himself ready for an 'end of time' of another kind, for an end which he is not condemned, but called upon, to *survive*.

Question: How do we know this? Answer: We do not 'know' this at all. But? But we are sure of it in the manner of faith. The proposition that 'there is no End in the absolute sense' can be legitimately laid down only on the basis of the concept of *creatio*, or rather on the basis of the belief that everything which is, is either *Creator* or *creatura*, and the human reality a creaturely reality. And all the dimensions of the concept *creatura* must be held in view. If one were to see only the *vertibilitas ad nihilum*, the proximity to nothingness, one would be more likely to come, on the contrary, to the conclusion that there may very well be, indeed there must be, a total annihilation of this 'decaying existence'; this is the natural end of the creature. This strange notion of 'creatureliness', from which the idea of the Creator is excluded, is, as we know, characteristic of one sector of existential philosophy. The full concept of creatureliness includes the provenance from the being-creating power of the Creator, who holds the *creatura* above nothingness with such an absolute strength of realization that this urge, to be, becomes simply identical with the inmost nature of the created entity. On the other hand, therefore, it must be seen, no, believed, that God has created things 'that they might be'.

No one can say there is no end of history in the absolute sense, unless he believes in the Creator.

[4]

How, then, are we to think of an 'end of history'? For what is meant is not something of the kind expressed in such notions as 'decline of the West', 'dissolution of an empire', 'relapse of a civilized people into the condition of fellaheen'. That would be shooting short of the target. We are speaking of the end of time and of history in a much more radical sense. We mean an End after which there will no longer be time or history. But if this End cannot be identical with total extinction and *annihilatio*—how can it be conceived?

It is necessary to return, once more, to the concept

creatio. However inconceivable this concept may be, the act of creation is certainly to be thought of as a *non-temporal* act, as taking place outside time, not occupying a given span of time (*sine motu et tempore*). [13] On the other hand, continuance in being through time, creaturely being, rests solely upon this non-temporal act of *creatio*: 'Maintenance in being does not happen through any new action' of God, [14] this 'maintenance' is the *creatio* itself. But this means that temporal-historical reality *in toto*, by virtue of its character of being creature, is situated in an absolutely immediate operational relationship to a *non*-temporal being and operating, in an uninterrupted and most intimate permeation, without which creature cannot be conceived (God is more inward to us than we are to ourselves, says Augustine). The average thinking of modern man may find difficulty in grasping this, because it is still moulded by the Enlightenment's notion of a purely extramundane God, of the *Deus extramundanus*, with whom is contrasted a finite world which is equally self-enclosed.

We really ought now to proceed to a more detailed discussion of the concept Time. But we shall endeavour to get along with naïve 'knowledge'—in the words of Augustine's *Confessions*: [15] 'As long as no one asks me, it seems to me that I know it; but if someone asks me and I have to explain it, it seems to me that I do not know it.' All the same, we must recall the fact that the 'untemporality' of the being and operation of the Creator possesses the character of eternity, bearing in mind that here 'eternity' does not mean, primarily, unlimited duration of time, but, in Boethius's phrase, which has entered into the Western tradition, 'the perfect and complete simultaneous possession of unlimited life'; or, as Thomas[16] puts it, 'Eternal is . . . that whose being is simultaneously the whole'; not succession of days, but always-now, *nunc stans*, the standing now, in which 'everything simultaneously' is reality.

It is therefore, this realm of the untemporal-eternal upon which human history, that happens through time, continually and immediately borders. The expression 'borders upon' is, of course, far too weak, indeed positively inapt: the temporal is inwardly sustained, saturated, pervaded by the untemporal. Because of this, the gaze of the man philosophizing about history does in truth fall as it were into a chasm (the same thing, however, happens in all philosophizing, in all reflective contemplation, whether it is revelation or historical reality itself that is contemplated—in so far, of course, as the enquiry is directed upon their roots!).

How is the end of history to be conceived? Revelation speaks of a New Heaven and a New Earth, which theological interpretation construes to mean that there will be a 'transposition' of the temporal being of the historical world into the state of direct participation in the untemporal mode of being of the Creator. Now, this 'transposition' cannot be thought of as brought about by any historical, temporal power. This can be stated purely on account of the concept 'creature'; it does not require an explicit exposition of the theological doctrine of incarnation (although it is self-evident that without the latter the idea of the New Heaven and the New Earth cannot be adequately comprehended, but this lies outside the province of our enquiry). The transposition of the temporal into the untemporal can be conceived only as effected by a direct intervention of the Creator. 'In the Apocalypse (10, 5) "an angel lifts up his hand to heaven and swears by him that liveth for ever and ever, who created heaven . . ., that there should be Time no longer"'—Immanuel Kant was still able to write thus with comparative *insouciance* in his pamphlet on *The End of All Things* (whereas one can hardly imagine the Revelation of St. John the Divine being quoted in a contemporary 'culture-sociological' philosophy of history).

The transposition into untemporality, as regards its How, can be the object of theological interpretation alone. He who philosophizes, even if he is otherwise formally prepared to refer back to the *depositum* of pre-philosophical tradition, can say nothing on this topic. For him it is, of course, of indirect importance that, and in what manner, the notion of a 'New Heaven and New Earth', in its secularized and degenerate shape, has become and remained an historical *agens* of the utmost significance. Of direct importance to the man who philosophizes remains, however, first: the theological pronouncement that such a transposition will take place and that the 'end of time' is to be thought of after this fashion. Secondly, however, and above all, he is concerned with the preparation of this transposition within history.

For it is an inseparable part of the pronouncement of the revealed prophecy of the end that the transposition, although it cannot be brought about by forces within history, is nonetheless not unconnected with the course of historical events. This prophecy implies, rather, that the historical process itself is pressing towards its end, that it evokes this transposition, so to speak; not, of course, as an *effectus*, but as a deliverance. The prophecy of the End seems to indicate that the dichotomy through which history was set in motion, and which permeates it from its ground, will at the End reach an extreme crisis, that accordingly the end of time, inwardly as well as outwardly, will be utterly catastrophic in character, and that history will debouch into its end as into a deliverance coming from outside (it does not come 'from outside', however, but from creation's innermost ground of being, which, of course, absolutely transcends creation).

Does the reader observe the great gain in profundity, in inner credibility, in existential significance which accrues to thinking concerning the philosophy of history through this incorporation of revelation? Does not a 'philosophy of history' that concerns itself with the bare formal categories of the understanding of cultures appear, by comparison, almost wholly without importance?

It has, in the meantime, become possible to formulate the subject of our meditation more precisely How, in philosophical reflection upon history, are we to conceive the end-situation within history (and also how has it been conceived in the past?), the last, the ultimate situation before the transposition? What will the world look like at the instant before the angel of the Apocalypse raises his hand for the vow that there shall be no more Time?

It is evident why a bare culture-sociological philosophy of history is unable to put this question at all, although the diagnoses and prognoses to which it attains provide a good deal of 'material' for an answer. The earlier type of philosophy of history still made no bones about expressly pondering the question of the end-situation. Kant, thirteen years after the *Critique of Pure Reason*, could write his treatise, *The End of All Things*. Yet in the answers of those philosophies of the eighteenth and nineteenth centuries the unfathomable dimension of the Apocalypse was, mostly consciously, overlooked and concealed. And thus, by their patent inadequacy and by their grotesque errors regarding the further course of history, these answers were contributory causes to the radical refusal of later philosophy of history even to ask that question: according to the rules of the game of 'progress', 'The text is suppressed in the name of the commentaries, and then the commentaries are suppressed'.[17]

This has, of course, not been able to prevent a more or less clear notion of the conditions that will prevail

at the end of history being present to the age's vital
sense of the future.

[5]

The sense of the future possessed by this our
present is, naturally, not uniform. Nevertheless a few
broad common trends may be discerned which are
common to all of them. Naturally enough, they
appear more readily demonstrable in the negative than
in the positive. Let us take a look.

'I love the generation of centuries to come. For
this is my most blessed hope, the faith, which keeps
me strong and active, that our grandchildren will be
better than we. . . . We live in a period of time in
which everything is working towards better days.
These seeds of Enlightenment, these mute desires
and aspirations of individuals for the improvement
of the human race, will spread and grow strong and
bear glorious fruit'—thus the young Hölderlin writes
to his brother immediately after the outbreak of the
French Revolution, round about 1790.[18] One may
venture the assertion that in the Europe of our times
there can hardly be one educated young person with
a notion of the future similar to that of Hölderlin;
one will come across but few people who possess a
judgement concerning the reality of history and at
the same time envy their grandchildren their good
fortune in being able to live in the 'centuries to come'.

We need not go back a century and a half, however,

71

and it is not necessary to confine ourselves to the rather exhalted formulations of an ardent twenty-year-old. In Rudolf Eisler's *Dictionary of Philosophy*, 1922 edition, we find in the article on 'History' the following sentence: 'As men, by their instinctive and volitional activity, actively remould the conditions of life, from which they increasingly emancipate themselves, they engender ever more, ever richer, finer, more harmonious culture (q.v.) and thereby educate themselves ever more actively, freely and consciously in the direction of the cultural idea of mankind, of pure and complete "humanity" (q.v.), and of the will to reason which realizes it.'[19] What is being said in these scholarly words? Men become increasingly the masters of the forces of nature, which they take into their service (up to this point the author would still meet with agreement today, though not without reservations); but in addition, by achieving this men also engender ever finer, richer, more harmonious culture (this would already be more vigorously contradicted), and beyond this, they 'thereby' realize more and more, through self-education, the idea of humanity. This unification of technological, cultural and moral progress, in which unity, moreover, the essential nature of history is supposed to consist—this opinion, seen from the experiences of the intervening decades, seems to us altogether contrary to the facts and almost touching in its naïvety. Who could still deem it worthy of discussion?

Should we not, on the contrary, concur with the

diagnosis of Christopher Dawson[20] who, in respect of this co-ordination of technology and culture, says: 'We have entered on a new phase of culture . . ., in which the most amazing perfection of scientific technique is being devoted to purely ephemeral objects. . . . It is obvious that a civilization of this kind holds no promise for the future save that of social disintegration.' In this utterance the present's real sense of the future is speaking. It already announced itself in far-seeing figures like the Spaniard Donoso Cortes, who in 1849 said: 'Mankind is hastening with great strides towards the certain fate of despotism. . . . This despotism will evolve a power of destruction greater and mightier than anything we have heretofore experienced' (4.1.1849). The aged Jacob Burckhardt could also be named. Likewise John Henry Newman, who speaks in a letter of the 'great prophesying' of a friend, which is apparently beginning to reach fulfilment: 'He asked, who would be the Goths and Vandals destined to destroy modern civilization. . . . He gave himself the following answer: The lowest class, which is very great in numbers and unbelieving, will rise up out of the depths of modern cities and be the new scourge of God' (Autumn 1871). The great Vladimir Solovyev in his last book, *Three Conversations*,[21] from the year 1900: 'I am of the opinion that progress, that is, noticeably accelerated progress, is always a symptom of the end'; the same book contains the 'Narration concerning the Antichrist', of which we shall have more to say later; in it there occurs a well-aimed remark concerning the century 'which was so advanced that it was even vouchsafed it to be the last'. Theodor Haecker prefaced his book on *Virgil, the Father of the West*, which first appeared in 1931, with the terrifying epigraph: 'In times like these, my friends, let us consider before it is too late what we shall take with us out of the horrors of desolation. Well then, as Aeneas took first the *penates*, so we shall take first the cross, whose sign we can still make before it crushes us. And then, well, whatever each of us loves most dearly. But let us not forget our Virgil, that goes into a jacket-pocket.' The sense of the future expressed in these words, which is certainly gloomy enough, would appear, scarcely two decades later, to have grown yet more hopeless by a not inconsiderable degree: one is no longer so sure that it will still be possible to find any place of escape from the horrors of desolation, or that one will be able (or wish) to take anything with one, let alone Virgil. 'The problem that mankind is facing is that of living in a world in which there seems to be no limit set to what man can do with his environment and with himself' is a statement in the very sober and thoughtful report[22] rendered by a commission of theologians, educationists, and scientists set up by the British Council of Churches 'to consider the problems created by the discovery of atomic energy'. This report also contains the sentence, 'We have, therefore, to reckon with the possibility that men may, in their folly or wickedness, blot out civilization or even, it may be, bring to an end the existence of the human race'. And Alfred Weber, who remarked on the supersession of Philosophy of History by Cultural Sociology, says in an essay on the inner situation after the Second World War[23], 'the outcome of history up to now is that mankind is returning to the dread of the world and existence that is felt by primitive peoples'.

Of course there are counter-voices raised in opposition to this chorus, but they do not carry much conviction, either because they are unconvincing from the outset (as, for instance, shallow, utilitarian optimism springing from political ideologies), or because they do not sufficiently consider the totality of history, but confine themselves to the province of technology —a reproach which must also be levelled against Friedrich Dessauer when he concludes his book on atomic energy[24] with the 'hope' 'that the favour of such immense power will finally compel the human world to order itself on justice and equity'. This kind of optimism does not penetrate to the depths at which our present's sense of the future has its origins.

But what is the purpose of assembling this testimony of pessimism? The first was to show, purely as a statement of fact, what has actually become of the Enlightenment's faith in progress, under the hammer of events themselves. This statement of fact does not imply that there was *nothing* in that faith in progress which corresponded to the truth of what really happens in history. Further, it does not imply that

75

pessimism is the true, objectively justified, or even the 'Christian' attitude to history.

All the same, in the revealed prophecy of the end of history a catastrophic end within history is foretold. Whoever believingly accepts this prophecy, that is to say, whoever takes it to be revelation, has no possibility of ignoring the fact that the end of Time, within history, will be a downfall, a catastrophe. None the less, his attitude to history, his attitude to the future, may not be one of despair—and this for reasons arising out of that very same faith. The hope of him who thus believes, of him who believes in the 'transposition' as deliverance, is by no means a hope directed purely upon the 'beyond'. It is, rather, a hope that renders the believer able and willing to act here and now, within history, indeed even to see in the midst of the catastrophe itself a possibility of meaningful action within history. Admittedly, this attitude, as really lived, can flourish only on the soil of that believing understanding of the end of Time—an end which, although catastrophic, does not mean disaster.

This is one of the reasons why today, at a time of temptations to despair, it may appear necessary to bring into view a notion of the End in which an utterly realistic freedom from illusion not only does not contradict hope, but in which the one serves to confirm and corroborate the other.

Extreme pessimism, by which this epoch's sense of the future seems above all to be stamped, must, as we have already said, be regarded as a symptom of the decay of the Enlightenment's doctrine of progress. And it is actually a fact that this reciprocal relationship between the former pessimism and the latter optimism is really still alive in contemporary consciousness; hence the contemporary world's sense of the future must be understood not exclusively from the point of view of the pessimism that stands in the foreground, but at the same time from the angle of the optimism with regard to events within history, which continues to be thought and is equally 'present'.

However, we are not really concerned with a 'cultural sociological' analysis of the *de facto* sense of the future carried to the limits of differentiation, but with the provision of an answer of the human understanding and heart to the question what, really and in the last analysis, happens in all history, that shall be as objectively correct, as 'true' as possible. In order, therefore, that the rights of optimism and pessimism as well as the very limited validity of these two concepts shall emerge more clearly, it is necessary first to adduce a few distinctions in principle.

In Latin the word for end—*finis*—also means goal. End and goal, however, are certainly not the same thing. There may be an end which is not simultaneously a goal. Something may 'cease' without having

77

reached its goal. There may be an end which is characterized precisely by the goal having been missed, an end which is synonymous with non-attainment of the goal. Nevertheless, goal and end inwardly cohere. I refuse—and in doing so know that my refusal is correct—I reject the idea that I ought to believe the world so constructed that it is leading to an end in which the goal is missed, and that, in other words, the name of the course of the world is 'futility'.

But how, in the Christian-Western tradition, in the notion of the end of history which characterizes it, is the correlation of *finis*-end and *finis*-goal conceived? This correlation is not easily grasped; it is complicated by the necessity of discriminating between an *intra*-historical and an *extra*-temporal end of history, segregated from one another by the act of transposition of the temporal into the extra-temporal. Thus the doctrine of the End that is rooted in tradition descries through the ultimate happening within history the act of transposition and the extra-temporal end of history effected by it. The end within history, so says revelation, is catastrophic in character, which must mean that it is not identical with attainment of the goal and with realization of the intention. However, this cannot be stated without reservations. In no case, according to tradition, can this end within history, however much it has been foretold as a catastrophe, be construed as a definitive failure to fulfil the intention—since the authentic and ultimate end only follows upon the end-situation within history; and it is only this end 'outside time' of which we can finally say whether *finis*-end and *finis*-goal coincide in it or not.

But how is this question to be answered? With a simultaneous 'Yes' and 'No'. But why not simply with Yes or simply with No? Because, according to the pronouncement of theology, after the final end of history there will, on the one hand, undoubtedly be the reality of irrevocable separation from the ultimate ground of being, the reality of disavowal, of damnation or whatever name may be given to this state of having missed the goal; because, according to this, there is an end which is not simultaneously attainment of the goal. But now for the 'on the other hand'! The theological interpretation states: even in the reality of disavowal, damnation, separation, the goal of the *creatio* will not, in the ultimate, most profound and inapprehensible sense, really have been missed.

But to the distinction between the intra-historical and the extra-temporal end, there still remains to be added the distinction concealedness-manifestness, in which the category of concealedness is to be correlated with the catastrophic end within history, and with the end outside time the category of manifestness, the rendering visible of the undiscernible, the destruction of appearances—otherwise expressed, the category of public verdict, of judgement. (Incidentally, the question immediately presents itself: appearances to whom, concealment from whom? These notions already contain the idea that both the semblance and the concealment are not absolute, and that there is an eye to which the concealed is manifest and by which appearances are seen through.)

Can it now be said, after this attempt to clarify the preliminary field of the concept, whether the answer given by a Christian-Western philosophy of history, *vis-à-vis* the conflict between the optimistic belief in progress and the pessimistic anticipation of disaster, tends towards the one or the other side? Will such a philosophy of history, in so far as it treats specifically of history, give an optimistic or a pessimistic forecast? It reckons with a catastrophic end-situation of history, it makes ready for the foundering of what may be called the 'will to culture', a foundering on a scale both so extensive and so intensive that salvage within history seems impossible. Pessimism then? No! For the end-situation within history is, firstly, not construed as the ultimately valid end. Secondly, it falls within the category of concealedness and unauthenticity. Precisely in this apparent failure to attain the intended goal, in this futility which alone is visible to finite cognition, authentic realization may be achieved under cover—just as the *per se* paradigmatic, in the highest, indeed absolute sense 'successful' event of history wore, within history, the disguise of utter futility. The designation 'pessimistic' is also inapt for the further reason than an extra-temporal end is hoped for, in which it will become manifest that there is no missing-of-the-goal in an absolute sense and that, despite the reality of the extra-temporal end-situation of rejection, the true name of the ultimately valid End, of course in an entirely incomprehensible manner, is: New Heaven and New Earth.

This structure, with its not inconsiderable complexity, is peculiar to all ideas concerning the end of history which are truly rooted in the Christian-Western tradition. It must not, of course, be forgotten that nothing at all has so far been said of certain components of the Christian view of history, e.g. of the demonic historical powers. This complication in no wise renders its historical thought contradictory, it does not even make it ambiguous. But it is this which gives the Christian view of history its tense and, at the same time, extremely spacious structure.

The medieval Western attitude to history, for instance, is marked, on the one hand, by the fact that the current present is construed as the era more or less immediately preceding the dominion of Anti-christ. In Augustine's books on the State of God[25] world history appears divided into seven aeons, 'In the sixth we are now living'. And the German, Anselm of Havelberg,[26] who, in the middle of the twelfth century, wrote a book on 'the uniformity of faith and the multiformity of life from the time of Abel the Just to the last one of the Chosen', speaks of the seven ages of history, deeming his own to be the fifth, while the sixth would be the era of Anti-christ. The same is true of Otto of Freising and other chroniclers. Nevertheless, there can be no suggestion that despair of the future determined the historical attitude of this same period.

This becomes clearer still if we cast our eyes upon the political sphere and consider that, for instance, the conception 'Holy Roman Empire of the German Nation' was, on the one hand, the epitome of the most intense activity within history, while on the other it was only conceivable through the fact that the eschato-logical character of this Roman Empire was explicitly understood and acknowledged. St. Jerome's com-mentary on the Book of Daniel had interpreted the prophet's prediction of the four world empires as signifying the Babylonian, the Median-Persian, the Macedonian-Hellenistic, and the Roman. Since that time the Roman Empire has been regarded in the West as the last. Thus for Charlemagne, as for Otto I, an authentic empire could exist only as the 'Roman Empire', which was 'transferred' now to the Franks, now to the Germans—an empire on the threshold of the Day of Judgement. We are not concerned here with a more detailed discussion of the content of this conception. Of importance to us is its formal structure: that, in face of an end of time explicitly conceived as catastrophic, namely as the dominion of Antichrist, people were able to live *without* any sacrifice of activity within history, which seems rather to have had its roots in a kind of metaphysical assurance and which shows itself in an incomparable power of building and founding.

The many layers of this attiude to history cannot be apprehended with the simplifying concepts 'optimistic-pessimistic'.

The statement made by—surprisingly!—Jacob Burckhardt,[27] is too simple: 'In the whole of Western Europe there persists the conflict that arose out of the French Revolution, and the Church, especially the Catholic Church; a conflict which, in the last resort, rests upon the optimism of the former and the pessimism of the latter'. There may be some justice in describing the world view of 1789 as 'optimism' (Burckhardt sees its salient features as 'acquisitive sense' and 'power sense'); although a more deeply penetrating analysis would perforce come upon despair as the ground that made this optimism possible. To style 'the Church's' attitude to history unmitigated pessimism, however, is an unwarranted simplification.

[7]

Such over-simplified characterizations become possible and, to some degree, meaningful, only when the tense and complex structure of the Western conception of history, and above all of the notion of the end of time, dissolves. This dissolution, by the way, does not imply the loss of all the individual elements of the old conception of history, for instance the most unequivocally religious elements stemming from the *depositum* of revelation. What has been lost is the bond between them, whose significance can be guaranteed only from a pre-philosophical tradition. When, for example, Herder[28] says that the realm of man's basic dispositions to humanity, and their development, is 'the authentic City of God on Earth', he undoubtedly means the perfection of mankind within history; but he designates it with a word which the *depositum* of revelation uses to describe the extra-temporal end-situation; Herder's formulation even contains the palpable implication that the name 'City of God' applies with less authenticity and force to this extra-temporal end-situation of perfection than to the intra-historical situation of realized humanity. It has been asserted further, with good reason, that the vision of the final goal contained in the Communist Manifesto is, in its elements, likewise related to, or even identical with, the image of the New Earth, as foretold in the revealed prophecy of the End.[29] Yet these concepts and images, 'City of God', 'New Heaven and New Earth', have their significant place only in so far as they enter into the unimpaired structure of the traditional view of history, in which all the individual elements are linked together: the transposition; the intra-historical and extra-temporal end-situations; the concealed or manifest attainment or non-attainment of the goal; the catastrophic character of the intra-historical end, upon which, and as a deliverance, the extra-temporal end ensues.

Only when the highly intricate structure of this conception of history—which answers to the intricate, indeed mysterious, structure of historical reality—dissolves, only then, as has already been remarked, will any such thing be possible as the straightforwardly 'optimistic' simplification of the philosophy of progress, on the subject of which a word now remains to be said. This new, over-simplified and optimistic conception of history began to force its way through with the Humanists of the 'Renaissance' centuries. The current present, then, was in no wise seen as the 'last' epoch before the kingdom of Antichrist; the present was seen rather as the latest phase in the approximation to perfection—conceived as occurring entirely *within* history—as superior to the past and as preparing the way for a still happier future. 'Happiness and salvation', said Francis Bacon, would be disseminated by the science renewed by himself, which he construed as wholly an instrument of progress within history, meaning by this pre-eminently progress in the sense of technological civilization, the enrichment of human life by fresh discoveries. This notion of a state of perfection within history forced itself through even in spirits like Giambattista Vico, who not only discerned with complete realism the manifold layers of historical reality, but regarded the decline of individual cultures as something wholly determined by the laws of nature (at the end of every culture there stands luxury and 'meditated wickedness', 'the barbarism of reflection'); even Vico assumes a fresh beginning after every such end, and an advance in the whole—till the end-situation within history of a Republic of Mankind ordered according to the laws of Reason, in which the idea of Justice will prevail. In the same eighteenth-century the Swiss, Isaak Iselin (1764), wrote his widely read *Concerning the History of Mankind* with the basic thesis that the Golden Age belongs not to the past, but to the future (the future within history, of course) and that history is an advance from artlessness to an ever higher degree of light, and finally to universal bliss (Schiller, a generation later, was to term this the path of mankind from Arcadia to Elysium.) Iselin's primitive simplicity may have been received ironically by many of his more perspicacious contemporaries, but at bottom no small number of his opponents were of entirely the same opinion as himself.

This is true, for instance, of Herder, who attacked Iselin and yet himself says: 'By the laws of their inner nature, with the passage of ages, reason and equity must gain ground among men and foster an enduring humanity'.[31] Now this idea of an 'everlasting advance of our kind' (Fichte) is ubiquitous; it dominated European thought and evoked 'all the ardour and faith of a genuine religion'.[32] Whether Kant speaks of a realm of true culture and perpetual peace (although Kant, being a truly great thinker, also discerned the counterpart of this idea—of which more will be said later); whether Friedrich Engels[33] prophesies that an organization of production will come, 'in which productive labour, instead of being a means to the subjection of men, will become a means to their emancipation, by giving each individual the opportunity to develop and exercise all his faculties, physical and mental, in all directions; in which, therefore, productive labour will become a pleasure instead of a burden'; whether Kalinin says, in a speech in 1933, that mankind is approximating, in the measure of Communist reconstruction, 'more and more to a new, really human society, with which history first really begins and understanding guides the world';[34] whether, finally, the Atlantic Charter speaks of a peace 'which shall guarantee that all men in all countries can live the whole of their lives free from fear and want'—in all these formulations the common idea of progress within history is still alive. This idea expresses the opinion that the historical process itself, with greater or lesser necessity, but in any case on the basis of forces operating within history, is leading to an end-situation 'in which all demands of a religious, moral, artistic, economic, and political nature are fulfilled'.[35] All these opinions rest upon the dissolution of the Christian view of history, from which the element of the catastrophic end within history has been expunged, while the notion of a 'City of God' outside Time has been completely inverted to re-emerge as the concept of an ideal social condition which can be realized within Time through cultural, political and economic progress (or, as Stalin[36] re-formulated this bourgeois term: forward march).

This simplification, whose inaptness is ever more remorselessly laid bare by the course of history itself, this optimistic abridgement, arose (and arises) out of an attitude which finds the road to an *extra*-temporal and *post*-historical 'New Earth', leading through a catastrophic End and a divine transposition, insufficiently 'evident' in theory and, above all, too arduous of 'political realization'. It has, *inevitably*, been answered by a retaliatory pessimism which, having lost its illusions regarding real history, is preparing for a catastrophic End; in equal, indeed even greater contradiction to the traditional notion of history, however, this End is construed as final, as a catastrophe beyond which no promise of deliverance is audible, no 'City of God' visible, as a catastrophe which is supposed, if that were possible, to possess the character of *annihilatio*.

[8]

It has been said that *Immanuel Kant* proved himself great in his historical thought by the fact that he also envisaged the *altera pars*. On the other hand, of course, one is inclined to wonder whether this very fact did not intensify the element of 'enlightenment', whether Kant, precisely because he maintained the idea of the perfectibility of the human race within history, *despite* his awareness of the arguments against it and in a kind of desperate self-exhortation, did not give new life to this 'enlightened' view of history. Let us look a little closer. Apart from anything else, it may be worth our while to penetrate, at one point, right down to the substratum and lay bare the successive layers in the intellectual structure of the philosophy of progress. Kant is of greater importance than all the rest, however, not merely because the doctrine of progress found in his work its most highly differentiated formulation, but also because, over and above all formal sequence and overt influence, he still determines the atmosphere of contemporary thought as a paradigmatic figure.

It was not till he had reached his sixtieth year that Kant began formally to express himself on the subject of history. And of the first treatise of this kind (*Ideal of a Universal History based on the Principle of World-Citizenship*), which appeared in 1784, he says himself[37] that it was extorted from him. Although the theme 'end of history' is more explicitly propounded in some of Kant's later works, it is none the less noteworthy that certain recurring components of his notion of history are clearly formulated here. 'The attainment of a civil society universally governed by justice',[38] 'an internally—and for this purpose also externally—perfect State constitution', this is the goal of the 'history of the human species as a whole' as the 'execution of a hidden plan of Nature'.[39] 'We see,' Kant adds to these propositions, 'we see that

89

philosophy too may have its Millennarianism'—with which remark the enlightener seems ironically to interrupt his own discourse; similarly, too, there is a great deal to suggest that he regarded realization of this ideal situation at the end of time as being possible only in an approximate fashion ('from such crooked wood as that of which man is made, nothing wholly straight can be carpentered').[40] Despite this—the very contradiction is characteristic!—he nevertheless states without reservation that 'enlightenment' will inevitably 'mount little by little to the thrones and even exercise an influence upon the principles by which they govern', and this affords 'hope that, after many reformative revolutions . . . a condition of world citizenship will finally . . . come to pass in the hereafter'.[41] The phrase 'in the hereafter' belongs, of course, to the language of religious promises regarding the End outside Time; but it undoubtedly refers to a condition brought about within history by human effort. It should, moreover, be noted how entirely positive is the construction, five years before the French Revolution, placed upon the concept 'revolution': 'by each revolution the seed of enlightenment . . . is more and more developed', so that 'a consoling vista into the future' opens up, in which the human species will 'at last work its way up to the condition in which . . . its destiny here on earth can be fulfilled'; this, however, will provide a 'justification of Nature—or, rather, of Providence'.[42] Here an astonishing idea is expressed: the assumption of continuous progress on the part of mankind appears in its theological function as an argument of theodicy. Yet this amazing idea is one of the original elements in the creed of progress. Kant formulated the same idea still more clearly two years later in his essay on the *Conjectural Beginning of Human History* (1786): It is of the greatest importance to men 'to be content with Providence', this contentment, however, is engendered by the knowledge that 'the course of human affairs' 'develops gradually from the worse to the better, to which progress, then, each one of us is called upon by Nature herself to contribute for his part as much as lies within his power'.[43]

How much the Enlightenment's doctrine of progress rested upon a secularization of Christian theology, more precisely, of the theology of the Last Things, is shown, in the very title, by the treatise *The Victory of the Good Principle over the Evil and the Establishment of the Kingdom of God on Earth*[44] (1792); we see at once that the language is the language of theology. But what is the content of this pronouncement framed in theological terms? What does Kant understand by the 'establishment of the Kingdom of God on Earth'? The answer is: 'The gradual transition from ecclesiastical creed to the absolute sovereignty of pure religious faith is the approach of the Kingdom of God'.[45] It is worth while considering for a moment what is meant here by 'ecclesiastical creed' and, above all, what by 'pure religious faith'. Ecclesiastical creed means the faith

91

lived in the *cultus*, the faith grounded on revelation, which treats of a history of salvation. And 'pure religious faith'? This is the bare faith in Reason, which, stripped of the *cultus*, is no more than morality. Yet the establishment of the Kingdom of God on earth is discussed in wholly concrete terms, concrete, that is, in an historical sense. The positively political character of this pronouncement, only slightly camouflaged because of the danger into which it might have placed the author, can be understood when one reflects that it was written with the French Revolution in view. This pronouncement was aimed at the French Revolution; this would be clear even if the previous sentence had not expressly mentioned revolutions 'which may shorten this progress'[46] from ecclesiastical creed to the faith of Reason. The establishment of the Kingdom of God on earth can, therefore, be put like this: 'If only the principle of gradual transition from ecclesiastical creed to the universal religion of Reason . . . has struck public root, in general or at some particular point, even though the real establishment of the same is still infinitely distant from us— this means: if the suppression of ecclesiastical creed by the religion of Reason has at some particular point, as for example in Revolutionary France, acquired "public", that is to say, State or legal, recognition— *then* "it may be said with cause that 'the Kingdom of God has come to us'"'.[47] The believer cannot help being shocked as he watches a fundamental concept of New Testament revelation being thus debased and inverted before his eyes into a crudely rationalistic formulation; moreover, even the non-believer of a later generation will look back in surprise at this shallow and over-hasty misinterpretation of the enigma of history.

Whether the Human Race is continually advancing towards the Better is the title of an essay written in the same year, 1792.[48] In this work the question 'Progress: Yes or no?' was answered as precisely as it was put, in brief sections formulated like theses ('What is it that we seek to know here?', 'How is it to be known?'). The point of departure is outlined thus: 'The cases that might be predicted are three in number. The human race is either in perpetual retrogression to the worse in its moral tone, or in continual progress to the better, or at an everlasting standstill at the present level of its ethical value amongst the components of creation'.[49] One of these three possible theses Kant immediately eliminates as beyond discussion, the first. This 'terroristic way of imagining human history' would imply that the human race might 'blot itself out'. This is, for Kant, an obviously unthinkable notion. (For us it is altogether thinkable; who today would regard as inapt the following proposition, which has already been quoted once: 'We have, therefore, to reckon with the possibility that men may, in their folly or wickedness, blot out civilization or even, it may be, bring to an end the existence of the human race'?)[50] The two remaining views ('progress to the better', or 'standstill') Kant leaves at the beginning more or less open; he rarely seems to have started out so 'free from preconceptions' as he does here. From this indecision,—and now the real argument begins—one can emerge only if an 'event' can be found in historical experience which contains a pointer as to the capacity of the human race to effect its own progress 'towards the better'. 'Therefore an event must be sought', which will point so strongly to the presence in mankind of a power of progress that we may, indeed must, infer 'progression towards the better as an inevitable consequence'. The sought-for event must do even more than this: it must 'prove the tendency of the human race as a whole', not only as regards the future (as *signum prognosticon*), but also as regards the past (as *signum rememorativum*).[51] The crucial question is, therefore: *Is* there such an event accessible to experience? If not states Kant's thesis, then the assertion of continuous progress towards the better cannot be maintained. He himself answers with Yes. Let us recall that these ideas were written in the year 1792. Is the sought-for event the French Revolution then? No, not the Revolution itself. The 'event' is the 'sympathy in wish', bordering on 'enthusiasm', which this revolution finds 'in the soul of every onlooker'; this sympathy proves '(on account of its universality) to be a character of the human race as a whole and at the same time (on account of its unselfishness[52]) a moral character of the same, at least in embryo . . ., which not only allows us to hope for progression towards the better, but is itself an example of such progress'.[53] (An interpolated recollection: Goethe spoke at that time of the approbation 'with which the human race frequently proclaims actions and events which are leading it to destruction'.)[54]

The contentual good, to which this approbation and this 'sympathy' apply is above all the following: the striving after 'a constitution which cannot be bellicose, namely the republican'. With this the amazing argument has reached its 'conclusion'. The sought-for 'event' has been found: 'I now assert that, even without the spirit of a seer, I can predict to the human race . . . its progression towards the better, which can never again be wholly reversed'. And the 'critic', who has prized loose and shifted back the boundaries of human knowledge, ventures— more than ten years after the appearance of the *Critique of Pure Reason*—the following conclusion: 'It is, therefore, not merely a well-meant proposition, commendable for practical purposes, but also one which, all unbelievers to the contrary, is tenable in the strictest theory, that the human race has always been progressing towards the better and will always continue so to progress.' 'Violence on the part of the mighty will gradually diminish, obedience to the laws will increase'; men will 'see themselves obliged first to render the greatest obstacle to morality, namely war, little by little more humane, then less frequent, and finally, in the shape of aggressive war, to abolish it altogether . . .'[55]—

and so on. Kant adds a concluding remark, in which he anticipates, himself, the doubts of 'unbelievers', in order once more to oppose to them, in solemn affirmation, his own confession of 'faith'. This 'conclusion' shows once more how very much aware he was of the counterpart of progress, and how very much his hope is a *spes contra spem*. It runs as follows: 'A physician who used to console his patients day by day with the hope of a rapid recovery—telling one that his pulse was beating more strongly, the other that his discharge, the third that his sweat, gave promise of improvement etc.—received a visit from one of his friends. How goes it with your illness, friend? was his first question. How goes it? I'm positively dying with improvement! I cannot blame anyone if, seeing the evil that arises from the State, he despairs of the salvation of the human race and its progression towards the better; only I place my trust in the heroic remedy which Hume cites and which might effect a speedy cure. "When now (he says) I see the nations at war with one another, it is as though I were watching two drunken louts struggling and striking one another in their china shop. For it is not enough that it will take them a long time to recover from the bruises they have inflicted on each other, but on top of that they will have to pay for all the damage they have caused." *Sero sapiunt Phryges*. But the afterpangs of the present war may extort from the political soothsayer the admission of an imminent turn of the human race towards the better, which is now already in prospect.' Kant could hardly have imagined how utterly ineffectual this argument would prove for our generation; he can have had no presentiment of what has become of the 'proposition tenable even in the strictest theory' of perpetual progress, of war becoming more humane, etc., in the eyes of this generation. Is there a single person today who considers it impossible that, on the occasion of the next military dispute, not merely a 'china shop', but the planet Earth will be destroyed? Whether Kierkegaard is right with his proposition that he who is deceived is wiser than he who is not deceived, is an open question; but it is indisputable that he who is deceived fancies himself wiser.

Yet there is also something profoundly inappropriate about this consciousness of superiority over the 'Enlightenment'. The resoluteness of the faith in progress, of this positively desperate hope, draws its vigour from a metaphysical root, the true meaning of which was admittedly invisible, or had become unclear, to Kant, but which is an essential part of the primal fund of a specifically human existence. And if our 'freedom from illusion' were to mean that connexion with this root had been cut, this 'realism of despair' would be further from reality than the Enlightenment's faith in progress, which seems to us naïve.

When the seventy-year-old Kant informed the editorial board of the *Berlinische Monatschrift*, in 1794, of his intention to send them a contribution on

The End of All Things, he wrote that the essay would be in part distressing to read and in part amusing. Again we are struck by this optimism softened— should we say, corroded?—by self-irony and scepticism, which, in this esoteric prefatory note, sets the subsequent pronouncement in a quite special key. Similarly, a year later, in the tract *Towards Perpetual Peace*, which achieved such fame, the unbroken trust expressed in the text itself ('perpetual peace' is no 'empty idea', but 'a task which, resolved little by little, draws continually closer to its goal, because it is to be hoped that the periods of time in which the same progress is made will grow ever shorter')—this optimism appears to be cancelled in advance and set in ironic quotation marks by the foreword, which tells of a Dutch innkeeper upon whose sign was 'painted a cemetery' with the legend 'Perpetual Peace', and asks 'whether this satirical legend . . . applies to human beings as a whole or particularly to the heads of States, who can never have enough of war, or to the philosophers who dream these sweet dreams'.

This cleavage and indecision, however much it may spring from a subterranean knowledge of the manifold stratification of the world, nevertheless has nothing in common with the tense and complex fabric of the Christian view of history. It is not as though hope of the New Heaven and the New Earth lost any of its decisiveness through the expectation of a catastrophic end within history; no, this hope is entirely unbroken despite the simultaneous preparedness for the world dominion of evil as the end-situation within history.

But now to turn to Kant's essay *The End of All Things*. A threefold notion of the end of things is possible, says Kant, and his exposition is subdivided accordingly. First, a 'natural' end of all things may be conceived; 'natural' implies, 'that which takes place necessarily . . . according to the laws of a certain order'. With the 'natural' is contrasted the 'non-natural', 'which may be either the supernatural or the counter-natural'. So that, besides the natural end, a supernatural and a counter-natural end are conceivable.[56] How then is the 'natural' end of things, that is, the end which takes place necessarily according to the laws of a certain order, to be thought of? It is 'naturally' the case, states Kant, that 'in the advances of the human race, the culture of talents, skill, and taste . . .' outruns 'the evolution of morality'.[57] This presumably means to say: It is natural that there is a span of time in which, amongst other things, achievements in the conquest of nature are, so to speak, devoid of ethical control. Speaking in even more concrete terms, it corresponds to the natural course of things that for a certain space of time mankind may handle atomic energy without yet being capable of applying it in conformity with 'morality', that is to say, meaningfully. Obviously, Kant cannot have visualized such extreme possibilities in the conquest of nature. But it is in relation to them that his principle first acquires a highly acute significance, since we have

to ask ourselves this: Will not this span of time—
whether it is ever bridged over by 'evolution' or
not—will not the span of time during which technical
power is not yet subordinated to moral guidance,
perhaps be too long, or at all events long enough
to make possible the effectuation of an 'end' which
Kant would scarcely have been willing to accept as
natural.

But we have interrupted Kant's train of thought;
the sentence quoted was an 'it is true that' sentence,
which must now be followed by its 'but'. 'It is true
that' the moral evolution of mankind naturally lags
behind its technological and civilizing advances: 'But
mankind's moral endowment . . . will hereafter over-
take them . . . and so one ought . . . according to the
proofs of experience that morality predominates in
our age to a greater extent than in any previous epoch
(here reference to the French Revolution is once more
unmistakable)—and so one ought (this is Kant's conclusion regarding the 'natural' end of things) 'to be
able to nourish the hope that the Day of Judgement
will make its appearance and bring about the end of
all things with an ascension of Elijah, rather than with
a journey to hell like that of the company of Korah'.[58]
The question of how it is known that mankind is really
growing ever more moral (it is not 'known', it is
'believed'!)—this Kant immediately evades: 'Here
we are merely dealing with ideas (or playing with
them), which the understanding creates for itself,
whose subject matter (if it exists) is situated far

above our field of vision.' Does this not again sound like an ironic, or else despairing, annulment of the whole argument? But it is no more than an interpolated exclamation, and the essay proceeds along its course.

The section on the supernatural or 'mystic' end begins with the sentence from the Apocalypse concerning the angel's vow, 'that there shall be time no longer'. 'If we are not to assume that this angel, "with his voice of seven thunders", was crying nonsense, he must have meant that there shall be change no longer.' This, however, is a 'contradictory notion that revolts the imagination', in the contemplation of which the brooding person falls into mysticism and becomes 'enraptured' (in the language of Kant, a highly censorious expression!), instead of, 'as beseems an intellectual inhabitant of the sensible world, keeping within the limits of this world'. The concept of 'eternal rest', this 'supposed blissful end of all things', seems to this enlightened spirit almost like a curiosity.[59]

Utterly astonishing, however, is what Kant has to say concerning the 'counter-natural', the 'topsyturvy' end of all things. First, he states, this end, in so far as it comes about, 'will be precipitated by ourselves, through our misunderstanding of the final purpose'.[60] It may be, let us recall, that this is only playing with ideas, which have perhaps no subject matter attached to them: all the same, in this play with ideas an end-catastrophe takes place which is brought

101

about by man as the subject of history! But how, in greater detail, is this end conceived. The notion is extremely bizarre. We must name the individual steps in the sequence of ideas: Christianity has something essentially lovable about it (Kant hastens to add the remark, which is profoundly characteristic of him: 'I do not mean here the lovability of the person who gained it for us by great sacrifices'!). This lovable element, however—namely, 'the liberal mode of thought', whereby Christianity 'is able to win for itself the hearts of men'—might perhaps one day be lost. But if this were to happen, 'if Christianity were ever to reach a point at which it ceased to be lovable', then aversion to Christianity would inevitably become the 'dominant mode of thought', 'and Antichrist would begin his rule (which is likely to be founded upon fear and self-interest); but then; because Christianity was destined to become the universal world-religion, but not so favoured by fate as to become so, the (topsy-turvy) end of all things, morally speaking, would come about'.

This is the last sentence of the whole essay. The mingling of Biblical, more exactly spoken Apocalyptic ideas with 'enlightened' notions and valuations is here so singular that it seems necessary to pause and consider this last passage. What does it actually say? It says: Christianity will (possibly) forfeit the sympathy of men by losing the lovableness specific to it, in other words, by being untrue to its own essential nature. The Apocalypse (and the New Testament as a whole) states exactly the reverse: The Church forfeits the sympathy of the overwhelming majority by the unadulterated realization of its essential nature. To be consistent, Kant would have to say that the 'great apostasy' of men who turn away from this degenerate Christianity is right. In the Apocalypse, the mass flight from the Church appears almost a confirmation of its truth; for the thought of the Enlightenment, it is, of course, an unthinkable idea that the truth may be fought although, or indeed because, it is the truth. Let us reconsider for an instant Kant's discrimination between 'ecclesiastical creed' and 'religion of Reason': The approach of the Kingdom of God on earth consists in the suppression of ecclesiastical creed by the religion of Reason—must not the contrary movement, then, the suppression of the religion of Reason by ecclesiastical creed, appear, conversely, as the approach of the Antichrist? This is not merely an abstractly proximate, or even an inescapable, consequence. Kant made the following explicit formulation: In that priests 'make observances and historical belief an essential duty' (by these he means public worship, sacrament, and belief in the events of the history of salvation), instead of 'taking to heart ethical principles', they are doing 'what is required to introduce him (Antichrist)'.[61] Thus the Antichrist appears as a positively ecclesiastical figure! Nevertheless, he is still under discussion, for the last time in the context of philosophy of history; until now, quite recently—an awkward and embarrassed silence having reigned throughout the whole of the nineteenth century up to the threshold of this present moment[62]—the possibility is discussed, in all seriousness and by no means 'rapturously', that 'a world organization might become the most deadly and impregnable of tyrannies, the final establishment of the reign of anti-Christ'.[63]

This is all meant by Kant, however, in the *modus irrealis*; just as in the treatise *Whether the Human Race is continually advancing towards the Better* the 'terroristic mode of representing human history' is only mentioned for the sake of systematic completeness, so here too the 'counter-natural', 'topsy-turvy' end of all things. Kant's true opinion, or rather the hope to which he desperately clings, is that the human race is really in the process of progressing continuously towards the 'natural' end, towards the establishment, within history, of the 'Kingdom of God on earth', effected gradually by historical forces, in which 'perpetual peace' shall reign and 'in which all seeds may develop to the full and accomplish their destiny here on earth'.[64]

In contrast to which, it is part of the pronouncement of the traditional Western view of history that at the 'end of all things' *all three* of those aspects will be realized which Kant—whether playfully or in perplexity—separated from one another, that of the 'natural', of the 'mystical', and of the 'topsy-turvy' end. At the end of history there will be a real amalgamation of the *fulfilment* of purposive striving within history, the transposition of temporality into participation in the eternal and timeless, into an *'eternal rest'*, and the final catastrophe within history of the reign of *Antichrist*!

The disintegration of this intellectually tensely-woven structure continues with strange consistency in post-Kantian historical thought. The disquiet which is still perceptible in Kant, the strain and desperation in his doctrine of progress, the irony which casts doubts upon his own statements, his realistic complexity of theory—all this gradually vanishes. Its place is taken by an unhesitating constructivism.

'In order to characterize correctly even one single age, including, if he wishes, his own, the philosopher must have understood *a priori*, and intimately penetrated, the whole of time and all its possible epochs'— Kant never uttered such exacting phrases. This, however, is the formulation contained in the first of the seventeen lectures on *The Basic Features of the Present Era*,[65] which *Fichte*, at the age of forty-two, delivered in Berlin in 1804–5. Fichte, undeterred by any theoretical hesitation, presupposes as accessible, and as known to himself, 'a world plan which can be clearly comprehended in its unity, and from which the major epochs of human life on earth may be completely deduced and descried in their origins and in their mutual inter-connexions';[66] 'this life on earth, with all its ramifications, can be deduced from the unitary concept of life eternal, which it is perfectly possible to envisage from this world below'.[67] One

105

can hardly believe that any one should have formulated such stupendous interpretations; and yet the continually recurring influence exercised by these intellectual fictions, above all in the domain of political ideologies and Utopias, must not be forgotten. Here we shall simply enquire how such thinking portrayed the 'end of history'.

'I therefore say, and in so doing lay the cornerstone of the edifice that is to be erected' (is this still the speech of a seeker after knowledge, of an enquirer, who is striving in silence to catch the answer of reality?) 'I say: the purpose of mankind's life on earth is that thereon it shall arrange all its affairs in freedom and according to Reason'.[68] From this emerges, for Fichte, the fundamental subdivision of the history of mankind; I must quote verbatim, since otherwise the reader will scarcely believe that a philosopher of such repute could be guilty of such frivolity. From this proposition, then, there emerge 'two great epochs': 'the one in which the species lives and is, without yet having arranged its affairs in freedom and according to reason; and the other, in which it achieves this rational arrangement in freedom'.[69] And the end of history? The goal of terrestrial life would have been reached, 'its end have appeared, and mankind would enter into the loftier spheres of eternity', when 'the art of arranging all the affairs of mankind according to Reason, having first been scientifically understood', had been so long applied to 'all the affairs of mankind' that the point had been reached when 'the species stands forth in Reason as a consummate impression of its eternal original'.[70] This, then, is Fichte's notion of the end-situation within history: 'The epoch of the art of Reason; the era in which mankind builds itself up with a sure and unerring hand to an accurate impression of Reason; the estate of consummate justification and sanctity'.[71]

It is a peculiarity of Fichte's conception that this notion of the end-situation is combined with a completely negative judgement on his own present, whereas in all other cases it has been part of the recurring scheme to interpret the current present as the highest stage of progress yet attained. Kant himself was no exception to this rule: 'If it be now asked which period of the known history of the Church up to now is the best, I have no hesitation in replying, it is the present, and so much so that nothing is needed now but to let the seed of true religious faith, as it has now . . . been publicly planted, develop more and more unhindered, to expect from it a continuous approach to that Church which will unite all men forever, and which constitutes the visible representation . . . of an invisible Kingdom of God on earth'.[72] Fichte on the contrary—who further subdivides his schema of the ages into five epochs, in which, to the accompaniment of conflicts, the end of time's 'estate of consummate justification' is realized—characterizes his own epoch, the third, as that of 'absolute indifference toward all truth, and complete unrestraint destitute of any guiding principles', as the 'estate of consummate sinfulness'.[73] Furthermore, frivolity is, so to speak, a guiding principle of this diagnosis also: '. . . so we make no enquiry as to whether the situation is really thus or not. If the situation is not thus—well, then we are not living in the third epoch'.[74] Or, even more amazingly, in the *Addresses to the German Nation*, of 1807–8, it is stated that the third epoch has 'within three years . . . come completely to an end and conclusion'[75]—though only in Germany! Yet, the notion of a 'City of God' within history is not only to be found amongst thinkers conditioned by the ideas of 1789. When *Novalis*, for instance, who is by the way an enthusiastic follower of Fichte, closes his essay *Christendom or Europe*, with the cry, 'Only have patience, it will, it must come, the holy age of perpetual peace, when the New Jerusalem will be the capital city of the world', he is thinking of the metropolis of a terrestrial-historical Christendom, which will arise 'out of the holy womb of a reverend Council of Europe'. And does the not infrequently heard statement, invoking Novalis, that a re-Christianization of Europe would also lead to a new political and cultural glory, not often enough mean a sort of 'City of God' within history? In this connexion, we must recall Augustine, who, after the fall of Rome, expressly opposed the 'apologetic and fawning self-advertisement of a Christian society',[76] which was at that time thinking, in terms of the same schema, that Rome, if it would only become Christian again, would once more achieve imperial power.

The constructivist element, which emerges in such an extreme guise in Fichte, is also to be found amongst representative Christian philosophers of history. *Josef von Görres*, who delivered his Munich lectures on *The Foundation, Subdivision and Temporal Sequence of World History* in 1830, disposes of the ages in a manner just as arbitrary as Fichte's, and of future ages too: 'The whole temporal passage of history is circumscribed in a sequence of thirty-six great divisions of time'.[77] Of course, Görres could construe the end within history no otherwise than as an appearance 'of all the dissonances of temporality'; nevertheless, he seems to take some of the seriousness of historical reality from this notion by speaking, in terms which, for our taste, are much too aesthetic, of the 'drama at the close',[78] or even of the 'sunset glow of the closing centuries, which plays in the tree-tops of re-established Eden'.[79]

What is more important than all else about the creed of progress is this: It is still 'one of the most powerful and practically effectual motive forces'[80] in the world—even if no longer in the sense given to it by Voltaire, who, alongside the 'improvement of morals', also numbered the *plaisirs de Paris* amongst the signs of progress,[81] though it is on entirely the same level when a recent popular work[82] sees 'the coming renascence of European civilization' guaranteed by, amongst other things, the provision of sports grounds and camping villages. Even the most reflective person, however, no matter how strong the

109

foundation for gloomy prognoses, will not easily bid farewell to the idea which has rightly been deemed to contain a formulation of 'the cultural sense of the Enlightenment', the idea that 'in a rationally ordered world, the rational man is faced with the task of organizing rationally his own affairs, his political and social life, in the certain hope that this is possible'. [83] None the less, it must be stated that this characterization of the situation of mankind acting in the world— seen from the viewpoint of the traditional Christian-Western conception of history—must appear to be, if not positively erroneous, at least incomplete.

The voice of faith in progress, which states that the end of history cannot possibly be total failure to attain the intention and goal of mankind, is answered by another that says: 'Out of such crooked wood as that of which man is made, nothing wholly straight can be carpentered' (as Kant puts it[84]). In more concrete terms, relating to the processes of history rather than to first principles, this second voice asks: Where can we discern any essential and continuous progress towards the shaping of social and political life by Reason? Has war really 'grown little by little more humane and less frequent', as is stated in Kant's 'proposition tenable according to the strictest theory'? Since comparative historical research reveals that civilizations never come to an end in any other fashion than by suicide[85], why should world civilization be an exception? In the face of this conflict of viewpoints, a true conception of history that corresponds to reality will have to be sufficiently spacious to accommodate what is incontrovertible on *both* sides. And if it is correct to say that throughout the parts of the world dominated by European thought the notion of history founded on the Enlightenment's faith in progress is still the one actually valid, then the prime necessity is to add to it the other dimension, readiness for a catastrophic end of time within history.

This does not mean that a true philosophy of history must be erected 'on the firm foundation of unrelenting despair';[86] this is precisely what it does *not* mean. Neither does it imply a renunciation of activity within history. It certainly does not signify that this present era, whose catastrophic features nobody will of course contest, must be construed as the 'end-period' in the exact sense.

What is meant is that the sempiternal proximity and permanent possiblity of a catastrophic end of time must be borne in mind.

Here, as Donoso Cortes put it, lies an especial opportunity for periods of catastrophe: Ages of uncertainty are those in which one experiences the greatest certainty of how one stands *vis-à-vis* the world.

CHAPTER III

[1]

In the tradition of Western historical thought, the end-situation within history is invariably entitled Dominion of Antichrist. It is therefore necessary to explain as precisely as possible what is meant by this expression.

The name 'Antichrist' may at first ring strangely on the modern ear. The meaning of this name in terms of historical reality is, however, very familiar to the contemporary man—to the contemporary man, which does not mean every man who is alive today on earth; it means whoever has observed and shared the experience of the most recently past events of human history (the totalitarian régime, 'total war' and its concomitants) with awakened senses and from within. That familiarity, which it will be easy to demonstrate, is something new. In the spiritual history of 'modern times' the notion of the Antichrist has met with the same fate as the whole notion of a catastrophic end-situation within history. It was looked upon as something belonging simply to the 'Dark Ages'.[1] Twenty years after Iselin's *History of Mankind*, synchronously with Kant's *Critique of Pure Reason*, the Swiss, Corrodi,

112

published a *Critical History of Millennarianism* (1781–1783), in the Preface to which he says, 'the history of mystical rapture is useful, because it preserves us from relapses', in addition to which it affords 'rich material for merriment'.[2] Has not the ingenuousness of this attitude of enlightened superiority assumed, in the interim, a touching character? This is equally true of the theology of this period, even of that which is in other respects ecclesiastically orthodox; in contrast to the 'exaggerations' of the medieval notion of the Antichrist, it laid great stress on adopting an emphatically enlightened attitude, which led it to adduce highly 'modern' arguments. Thus the important ecclesiastical historian Döllinger, for instance, points to the 'geographical expansion of our field of vision', in order to prove how difficult it is to imagine a persecution of the Church extending over the whole earth.[3] 'A world power which closes all churches in all parts of the earth and on every island simultaneously'[4] is for Döllinger 'something positively unthinkable'.[5] In the meantime, this 'unthinkable' idea has become completely familiar to us; few things enjoy such good prospects of successful operation as this technologically registerable simultaneity all over the planet, including the 'islands'. Above all, there is no trace today of the amused superiority which the century of the Enlightenment felt with regard to medieval notions of the *barbarity* of the Antichrist régime, which was simply dismissed as primitive fantasy. Contemporary man cannot escape

113

the feeling that, in some uncanny way, it 'all fits in' when, for example, he learns that according to the medieval tradition Antichrist brings with him a cremation furnace[6]—a notion which the enlightened narrator found as primitive as it was amusing.

[2]

What then, in detail, does the notion 'Dominion of Antichrist' imply?

It has already been mentioned that the more a philosophic enquiry relates to history, the more the enquirer needs to return to theology. In addition, the more closely a concept of theology is related to the Last Things, to the realization of the meaning of history, to the End, the more the totality of theological concepts comes into play. With respect to our theme, this means that a correct interpretation of the concept 'Dominion of Antichrist' presupposes that all the basic concepts of theology, or rather all the fundamental realities of the history of salvation, are correctly understood.

It presupposes, for example, that there are demonic powers in history. This is not to be construed in a vague, journalistic sense. 'Is there anyone who, although he believes that there are "horse matters", does not believe that there are horses, or, although there are "demonic things", there are no demons?'— to this question of Socrates[7] one may answer: Yes,

114

there are people who, although they talk about demonic things and persons, would never admit that there are demons. 'Demonic powers in history' means then, that there are demons, purely spiritual beings, fallen angels, at work upon human history. Not that the Antichrist is to be thought of as such a purely spiritual being; this is just what he is *not*. But in order that this phenomenon may be conceived as possible at all, in order that it can be said what the Antichrist really is, the existence of 'the Evil One' as a purely spiritual being must be accepted. Moreover, he must be accepted as an *historically powerful* being, indeed as the 'Prince of This World', in even more extreme terms, as the 'God of This World' (II Cor. 4, 4). (Here the theological interpretation of the material of tradition is far from providing us with adequately formulated notions; this is true particularly in respect of the historical power of the 'Prince of This World', a designation of which Raïssa Maritain[8] rightly says that it can hardly be 'no more than a divine irony'. Christ in no wise corrects the Tempter, when he shows him the kingdoms of the earth with their glory and says, 'All that is delivered unto me; and to whomsoever I will I give it' (Luke, 4, 6). Similarly, according to the Epistle of Jude (9), even Michael 'durst not bring against Satan a railing accusation'.) It is necessary, above all, to think the concept 'purely spiritual being' with all its consequences, unimaginable as it naturally is. Otherwise one misses the status and the incomparability within the realm of being, in respect both of intelligence and energy of will, which are to be ascribed to these demonic historical powers, in whose service we are to think of the Antichrist as being. It is not that the 'Prince of This World' is the Lord of History, but, as Theodor Haecker put it, 'he hastens its course; and that is the partly manifest, partly secret happening of our own day as of all days upon the whole world'.[9] An immense addition to the difficulties of all philosophy of history, there is no doubt of that! Nevertheless (this is Theodor Haecker again), 'there is nothing of which the true thinker and investigator has more dread than of omitting something which is real . . . The ruin of European philosophy of history . . . was the loss of this dread'.[10]

Furthermore, one understands nothing of the traditional notion of Antichrist unless one simultaneously thinks that there is a guilt which happened in primordial times and whose effects are at work upon historical ages, that there is original and hereditary sin. Notwithstanding the extent to which we are dealing here with a *mysterium* in the strict sense, which can never be resolved or rendered intelligible, without this assumption history acquires a positively absurd appearance. In no case, however, can the traditional notion of Antichrist be visualized without this pre-assumption, since the Antichrist is thought of as the phenomenal form of the most extreme radicalization of that 'discordancy' which entered into the historical world through original sin.

The Christian notion 'Dominion of Antichrist' is, moreover, not intelligible if it is not simultaneously conceived that original sin has been vanquished by the Logos become man, who *eo ipso* is also simultaneously the vanquisher of the Antichrist. We understand nothing about the Antichrist if we do not see him, despite all his power within history, as one who is fundamentally already defeated.

We do not understand the Antichrist, if we are not clear about the fact that the meaning of history is not 'culture'.

We must also know, for example, what a 'martyr' really is, and the fundamental meaning of the blood testimony. When, for instance, E. R. Curtius, writing of Toynbee's *Study of History*,[11] speaks of the Christian Churches and asks the question, 'Are they reserved for a martyrdom that might save us from technocracy?', it is true that the first part of this interrogative sentence corresponds entirely to the inner structure of the end-situation; but the second part of the question—whether the martyrdom of the Churches might perhaps 'save us' (whom actually?) from technocracy—this relative clause seems to indicate that the factors of the end-of-time situation have been seen in an altogether false light, so that the theological figure of the Antichrist, if any cause at all were found to introduce it into the historical play of forces as a particular figure, could not be correctly construed.

Once more, what is stated by the notion of the Dominion of Antichrist as the end-situation within history?

First of all it states, *per negationem*, that in the last analysis the real theme of world history is not, as Goethe put it,[12] belief and unbelief and the struggle between these two, but that, much more concretely, its theme is the struggle around Christ: if the figure which dominates history at the end of time is the Antichrist, then a figure which refers unequivocally to Christ is the principal actor of the last epochs. One may conjecture that this assertion will sound a great deal more significant to the contemporary man (as defined above) than it would have done to even a 'Christian' Liberal of the nineteenth century. The assertion means that history does not take place in a neutral province of 'culture' and what pertains to culture, and that 'the "neutrality" of the liberal outlook upon Christ can never be more than a passing phase' (Erik Peterson in his essays on eschatology).[13] In the nineteenth century it may, perhaps, have looked as though Christianity would be gradually forgotten, as though the world might one day see a purely profane culture —'profane' in the sense of being neutral, of leaving Christianity out of discussion. It may still look like this today, in so far as the issue is not the immediately 'existential' elements of life, but the mediate and less obligatory provinces of 'culture' (literature, art, *circenses*, economy). As soon, however, as these regions are subsumed under the much more 'existential' category of the exercise of political power, discussion suddenly centres very emphatically, indeed almost exclusively, round Christianity—seen, to be sure, as a power of resistance, of 'sabotage'. In Christian terms, it is Christianity as the *ecclesia martyrum* that is meant.

Just as the martyr, historically speaking, is a figure of the political order, so too the Antichrist is a phenomenon of the political sphere. The Antichrist is not something resembling a 'heretic', who is of importance only to *ecclesiastical* history, and to whom the rest of the world need pay no attention whatever. *Potentia saecularis*, worldly power—this, says Thomas,[14] is the specific instrument of the Antichrist; he is a worldly potentate. Tyrants, in their persecutions of the Church, Thomas states further,[15] are prototypes (*quasi figura*) of the Antichrist. The latter, then, is not conceived as a phenomenon on the brink of the historical field; rather is the Antichrist, in so far as history is primarily *political* history, an eminently historical figure.

This also implies that the End will not be chaos in the sense that the opposition and conflict between numbers of historical powers will cause a progressive dissolution of historical ties and structures, and finally putrefaction. On the contrary, the End will be characterized by one single governmental structure equipped with prodigious power, which, however, fails to establish any *genuine* order. At the end of history there will be a pseudo-order maintained in being by the exercise of power. Nihilism, *because*, unlike anarchism, it is distinguished by a 'relationship to order', 'is more difficult to see through, better camouflaged'—this perspicacious observation contained in the diagnosis of Ernst Jünger,[16] holds a very strong, though concealed, eschatological reference. The description 'pseudo-order' is also valid in the sense that the 'illusion' is successful; it is an element in the prophecy of the End that the 'desert of order' of the Antichrist will be regarded as a true and authentic order. The notion of a purely organizational social integument, in which everything 'technological', from the production of goods to hygiene, 'functions smoothly', and which is nevertheless fundamentally a phenomenon of disorder, is not very remote from contemporary experience. Perhaps the pseudo-order of the Dominion of Antichrist, after a 'period of chaos' on a vast scale, such as, in Toynbee's view, always precedes the establishment of a universal State, will be greeted as a deliverance (which would exactly confirm the character of the Antichrist as a pseudo-Christ).

The Antichrist is to be conceived as a figure exercising political power over the whole of mankind; as a *world ruler*. Once, and as soon as, world dominion in the full sense has become possible, the Antichrist has become possible. To this corresponds the other, co-ordinate fact that the Christian gospel must have reached the totality of the peoples of the earth, who have been rendered accessible to it politically: 'This gospel of the kingdom shall be preached in all the world for a witness unto all nations; and then shall the end come' (Matth. 24, 15)—which is not construed by theology to mean that the Christian religion will spread in triumph over the whole earth, but that the decision for or against Christ will become possible (or urgent) over the whole globe.

Here a misunderstanding must be eliminated: The traditional doctrine of the Antichrist does not include any possibility of knowing the date of the end of time; nor does it state that there can be no world dominion save that of Antichrist! The establishment of a World State, which is today well within the bounds of historical possibility, may quite possibly come to be looked upon as a legitimate goal of political endeavour. What this doctrine does state is that once this step has been taken mankind will find itself in a condition in which the Dominion of Antichrist has become more acutely possible than ever before: 'a world organization might become the most deadly and impregnable of tyrannies, the final establishment of the reign of anti-Christ',[17] (we have quoted this once before).

Seen from this angle, another pronouncement concerning the Antichrist, likewise contained in tradition, takes on a special appearance. The Antichrist will realize upon the earth a prodigious increase of power, and that not only *extensively*, but also *intensively*. The World State of Antichrist will be in the extreme sense a *totalitarian* State. This is determined however, not only by the lust for power and the *superbia* of the Antichrist, but at the same time by the nature of the World State itself. To become overnight a totalitarian State—that is the inner peril, arising directly out of its very structure, that threatens a World Empire, which, *per definitionem*, is devoid of neighbours and thereby unexpectedly conforms to the political islands of the Utopias. Thus the liberal Gibbon said of the *Imperium Romanum* that within it freedom could have been torn up by the roots 'because there was no possibility of flight'; 'if dominion fell into the hands of one individual, the world became a safe prison for his adversaries'. To this a diary of the last war[18] adds the conclusion that the objection can be raised to the 'unitary organization of the world', which is certainly imminent, 'from the standpoint of liberty, that it will leave no place to which one might emigrate'. The Kantian ideal of the abolition of truly 'external' wars, which would be attained in a World State, has its reverse side: the place of external wars would be taken by internal 'police actions', the character of which would approximate very closely to the extermination of pests.

This tendency of a world organization to become 'totalitarian' in consequence of it structure, has been frequently characterized—the evaluation given to it having been just as often positive as negative. There is Lenin's dictum: 'The whole of society will be *one* office and *one* factory, with the same work and the same wages';[19] there is an 'organizational socialism' which hails the 'world labour army' as an already imminent phenomenon. There are, on the other hand, the utterances of the aged Jacob Burckhardt to Friedrich von Preen, which speak of the 'great future authority' which nobody knows and which does not yet know itself, but for which all-levelling radicalism is preparing the way;[20] there is the pronouncement of a modern politician[21] that 'The world is developing in the direction of an absolute centre of power, a universal absolutism'. And as regards the prospects of the 'resistance of liberty', the conjecture has already been expressed, and it will doubtless find an echo in the sense of the future of many discerning contemporaries: 'Out of every struggle for the preservation of liberty, the substance of liberty emerges in some measure diminished, because, in order to be able to defend it effectively against its foes at all, a part of it must be surrendered, and this part is never again recovered.'[22]

It is of the essence of an *Imperium*, which encroaches upon existing kingships and nationhoods, and of the essence of the Caesar (says Erik Peterson),[23] that institutions are burst asunder, that the forms of social life rooted in tradition are dissolved and replaced by freshly erected constructions and forms; this can be gathered from the inner structure of the *Imperium Romanum* (the Jews say, we have no king but Caesar). But because 'in the *Imperium* the basis of all institutions' has been abandoned,[24] a situation arises in the religious sphere as well, indeed above all, which is new in principle. The notion of the controversy between Church and State, 'which confront one another as institutions and which, as institutions, must find a *modus vivendi*'—this notion, says Peterson, loses its validity in the *Imperium*. There is no longer controversy, but 'conflict': 'The cult of the old States could afford to be tolerant, the cult of the emperor had necessarily to become intolerant'.[25] This analysis, which strikes a target far beyond its immediate theme, provides a pointer to the internal situation of a World Empire at the end of time, whose prefigurations are by no means unfamiliar to contemporary man. The very structure of the World Empire seems to bring with it, as a kind of negative opportunity, the likelihood that the public position of the Church will change, as though by an automatic redirection of current. The possibility of penetrating and moulding public orders from the spiritual sphere will *cease* to exist; but a coercive power at the highest level of intensity, and not restricted by any bonds of tradition, will confront the Church in its rôle of *ecclesia martyrum*.

This danger, which is determined by objective circumstances themselves, will then—so runs tradition —be kindled to its extreme realization by the *person of the Antichrist*, who comes in the name of the angel who fell through his *will to power* and in whose 'ego-proclamations the history of human auto-apotheosis reaches its demonic acme'.[26] Precisely *because* of his extreme claim to power Antichrist will be accepted:

'If the other shall come in his own name, him ye will receive' (St. John 5, 43).

[4]

In the Apocalypse (13, 1f.), the Antichrist appears to St. John as a beast that rises up out of the sea—and moreover not as a beast known to experience, but as a monster (ten horns, seven heads, like unto a leopard, the feet of a bear, the mouth of a lion). The man who is at home, or thinks himself at home, in the realm of the 'humanistic', the so to speak classical man, has always felt this to be something insulting to the imagination and grossly absurd; one has only to read what Goethe wrote to Lavater concerning the latter's book on the Apocalypse. But perhaps such monstrosities may be comprehended with less difficulty by 'post-Goethean', modern man, who is not only familiar with Darwinism, the idea of human racial breeding,[27] and formulations such as those of Nietzsche and Spengler concerning the 'blond beast' and the human beast of prey, but has also seen the absolutely inhuman at its most extreme in empirical reality— all of which in conjunction finds expression in the monstrous shapes with which the visual arts and the poetry of today are populated. It is already partially intelligible to contemporary man that a 'planetary despotism with progressive technical development and the extinction of spirituality'[28] cannot be visualized in any other way than by the harsh unfamiliarity of such shapes as these, which are neither human nor animal. Theological interpretation construes the pronouncement of the Apocalypse entirely after this manner: as a visualization of human apostasy, which also puts away from itself the natural likeness to God ('We do not wish to be what God has called "Man"'),[29] as a characterization and unmasking of the 'cunning, coarse, all-devouring empire, of the world power that is governed by bestial instincts and comes to life in bestial shapes'.[30]

The Apocalypse speaks further of the second beast, bearing the same relation to the first that propaganda does to the exercise of power. Of this second beast, which embodies the prophet of Antichrist, it is said that he was 'like a lamb, and he spake as a dragon' (Apocalypse 13, 11). The two figures exercise in conjunction the total world dominion of evil, which reaches across the planet. 'And power was given him over *all* kindreds, and tongues, and nations' (13, 7); and 'all the world wondered after the beast' (13, 3).

Wondered at what? The Antichrist, who calls himself the God-man,[31] appears 'as though wounded to death; and his deadly wound was healed' (13, 3). And it is to this above all that the Antichrist's 'priestly propaganda'[32] points; this 'perverted gospel of Good Friday of the deadly wounding and miraculous healing of the Antichrist' is its 'favourite theme'.[33] The inverted *imitatio Christi*, the 'imitation' of the true Lord, here reaches its most extreme point.

The Apocalypse says the second beast causes 'the earth and them which dwell therein to worship the first beast, whose deadly wound was healed' (13, 12); it says 'to them that dwell on the earth that they should make an image of the beast, which had the wound by the sword and did live' (13, 14). Does not this formal structure (purely formally, 'miraculous deliverance' of the potentate) sound thoroughly familiar to us? But it must be borne in mind that it was also part of the antique cult of the emperor to believe, as a religious duty, in the *fortuna imperatoris*.[34]

Furthermore, tradition also sought to discern an objective feature of the Antichrist's resemblance to Christ in the fact that he will be a Jew; the Talmud itself sees him as a Jew.[35] Thomas Aquinas likewise repeated this opinion (*dicunt quidam* . . .): ' . . . and therefore the Jews will be the first to receive him and they will rebuild the Temple in Jerusalem, and so the words of the prophet Daniel will be fulfilled, "There will be in the Temple abomination[36] and an idol".'[37]

Here we must not suppress a remark concerning the eschatological rôle of Jewry. Anyone on watch for the more profound 'signs of the times' must always keep in view what is happening in the world to the Jews as a whole. And at the present time something truly exceptional is happening. We may think either of the antisemitism that is sweeping the world, the eschatological meaning of which has been interpreted as: 'that the Jews . . . are being compelled to recognize themselves as a special people . . . that the Jews

127

are being set more clearly than at any other time before the question of a terrestrially unprofitable conversion to Christ';[38] or we may observe the fact that in our day, for the first time since the Old Testament era, the State of Israel has once more given itself a national constitution; or we may think of the strange petition[39] which thereupon reached the Jewish Supreme Court in Jerusalem, asking that Israel, having recovered its sovereign Statehood, should undertake a 'legal review' of the trial of Jesus. In any case, 'the destiny of the Jews in the political world is ultimately not to be understood in the political, but in the theological sphere'.[40] And it is general theological doctrine that before the intra-temporal end of history, Jewry as a national totality will be converted to Christ—so that individual theologians have numbered amongst the factors which are still 'holding up' the End and the appearance of Antichrist, and which must first be removed (as St. Paul wrote to the Thessalonians, who were prematurely reckoning with the 'End'),[41] the persistent unbelief of Israel[42] (medieval theology, in this connexion, was thinking pre-eminently of the power for order of the Holy Roman Empire of the German Nation).

Further, tradition sees in the imitation of Christ only the extreme intensification of the mendacity and sham-sanctity which, in general, characterize the Antichrist. This latter term must be taken very exactly. What is involved here is not the famous 'cloak', but a total habitus extending into the province of the ethical, which must almost necessarily 'seem' to be real sanctity—in a world to which the original ontic and religious meaning of this concept has become unrecognizable. Only through this deceptive imitation of genuine sanctity, which even deceives the 'earnest', indeed the believers, does the perplexity of the many and, 'if it were possible, even of the chosen' become to some extent intelligible; here is something of the 'strong delusions', of which it is stated in the New Testament that God sent them 'that they should believe a lie' (II Thess. 2, 11). This power of deception, tradition[43] therefore sees as being founded primarily in the seeming sanctity of his personal life, over which Antichrist takes great pains. In the famous *Narration concerning the Antichrist*, which claims to present everything 'which can, with the greatest probability, be said on this theme according to Holy Scripture, ecclesiastical tradition, and sound common-sense',[44] Solovyev describes the Antichrist as a 'great spiritualist, ascetic and philanthropist', whose exalted self-esteem seems to be justified by the 'highest expressions of abstinence, unselfishness and active helpfulness'; he is 'above all others a compassionate friend of man, indeed not only a friend of man, but also of animals; he is himself a vegetarian'.[45]

It is part of the traditional picture of the Antichrist that he appears as a 'benefactor'; and at audiences he is 'so courteous that his courtesy will be spoken of in every broadsheet' says the *Life of Antichrist* written by a seventeenth-century Capuchin.[46] The Antichrist of Solovyev's legend is the author of a book that has that has been translated into all the major languages entitled *The Open Path to Peace and Prosperity throughout the World*. He has 'created a firmly grounded equality in all mankind: the equality of universal satiety'. And after he has been proclaimed ruler of the world—on the strength of an election without votes—the Antichrist issues a manifesto which concludes with the following words: 'Peoples of the earth! The pledges have been fulfilled! World peace has been secured to eternity. Every attempt to disturb it will instantly encounter insuperable resistance; for from this day forth there will be upon the earth only one single central power . . . This power is in my hands . . . International law at last possesses the sanction it has hitherto lacked. Henceforth no power will have the temerity to say "war", when I say "peace". Peoples of the earth! Peace be with you!'[47] Thus Solovyev in the the last year of the nineteenth century.

The power character of the dominion of Antichrist stands out particularly clearly in the last sentence of the manifesto. Theologians speak of the 'strongest world power in history'.[48] (We would call to mind the strange circumstance that Karl Marx sees the end-situation within history determined by the fact that 'there will be no more political power properly so-called'.[49] This becomes intelligible only on the assumption that here the end *outside* time, the 'City of God', is drawn into history. In historical reality, on the contrary, the intensified exercise of political power is everywhere intimated; Alfred Weber[50] sees the present condition of the world characterized by the fact that 'there are now only *de facto* relationships', 'which are becoming pure power-relationships'.)

In the 'consummation of the military, political, and economic merger in the religious united front',[51] the power of the Antichrist finds its most extreme intensification. The object of the religious cult is the world ruler himself; 'all the inhabitants of the earth, with the exception of the Chosen, pray to the beast and say: Who is there like unto the beast';[52] the possibility of emigration, even of 'inner emigration', disappears. There is no more neutrality.

This is, above all, the achievement of the 'priestly propaganda', which sets men in bewilderment by astonishing, miracle-like signs—in which connexion it has been remarked that this might refer to a 'social miracle'.[53] Above all, however, the prophet of the Antichrist organizes his cult (of which, by the way, Jung-Stilling,[54] the friend of Goethe, was already able to write in 1805 that this kind of 'divine service' would have to be military in character). The cult-image of the world ruler must be worshipped; this cult-image is 'an instrument of State politics, with which the friend is recognized and the foe revealed and brought to punishment. The "spirit" of the "image" finally represents the living canon for the judges of the empire'.[55] The political power which sets itself up as absolute carries out a 'total seizure' of the contents of existence and lays claim to the whole man, precisely to the domain of his personal religiosity, by simultaneously taking possession of the individual's immediate physical existence through an economic boycott. In the words of the Apocalypse, it is 'both small and great, rich and poor, bond and free' (can the absence of any exception to the 'seizure' be more clearly expressed?)—it is really 'all' who are brought by the prophet of Antichrist 'to receive a mark in their right hand, or in their foreheads, and that no man might buy or sell, save he that had the mark, or the name of the beast or the number of his name'. 'Fear and self-interest', as Immanuel Kant knew,[56] are 'likely to be' the foundation of the Dominion of Antichrist.

According to the unanimous information of tradition, the outward 'success' of this régime will be immense; its success will be a great apostasy. The fact of this mighty outward success distinguishes the Antichrist from Him to whom his name points *per negationem*. A theological commentary on the Apocalypse states: 'As in the days of Jesus of Nazareth, Herod and Pilate, Pharisees and Sadducees were drawn into friendship by their enmity to Christ, so in the days of the Antichrist everything that is called World will unite against the *Ecclesia*.'[57] *The* enemy of the World will be the Church; Thomas Aquinas seems to cast the circle still wider, one might almost

132

say more hopelessly, when he says, 'that final persecution', whose prototypes are the 'persecutions of the Church in this age', will be directed 'against all good men'.[58]

The final form within history of the relationship between the State and the Church will not be 'controversy', and not really 'conflict', but persecution, that is to say, the combating of the powerless by power. The way in which victory will be won over the Antichrist, however, is by the blood-testimony.

CONCLUSION

This is the notion of the end-situation within history grounded in Christian-Western tradition. Nothing is more natural than to find this notion terrifying. And nothing is more understandable than the wish simply to drive such thoughts out of one's head. Let him who can do this, do it. If a notion of the end of history is thought at all, then for the Christian no other is possible.

Of course, the prospect of the end-situation *within* history cannot be detached from the total body of the Christian-Western notion of the end of time. This notion includes the transposition out of temporality into participation in the eternity of God, the Judgement, and extra-temporal consummation, the 'City of God'. The Christian historical conception of the end of time includes the view *that Antichrist will be defeated*.

In the visions of the Revelation of St. John the Divine (Chap. 19, 11 ff.) heaven opens and releases a rider upon a white horse, 'clothed with a vesture dipped in blood: and his name is called The Word of God'. At the same time there appears 'in the sun' an angel, who cries to the birds, 'Come and gather yourselves unto the supper of the great God; that ye may eat the flesh of kings, and the flesh of captains, and the flesh of mighty men'. 'The beast, and the kings of the earth, and their armies' assemble for the decisive battle against the rider upon the white horse, of the issue of which it is reported only that Antichrist was taken 'and with him the false prophet that wrought miracles before him, with which he deceived them that had received the mark of the beast, and them that worshipped his image. These both were cast alive into a lake of fire burning with brimstone'. This end comes, so to speak, unannounced: the downfall takes place just as the power of Antichrist has reached its peak. In Solovyev's legend, the Antichrist has spoken immediately previously, before the World Council of Christians of all denominations, which has gone over to him, of the dawning 'great new epoch of Christian history'.

Yet is it not true that this idea of a catastrophic end is stark hopelessness and the gloomiest pessimism, which must serve to paralyse all activity within history?

The fact is, hope as a virtue, that is to say, as a quality of rightness in man, is a *theological* virtue—in so far as hope is understood in the sense of the Christian-Western tradition. This means that while justice, prudence, or courage may very well be natural virtues of natural man, hope is a virtue *only* when it is a *theological* virtue; hope becomes a virtue precisely through that which renders it theological, supra-natural virtue.

It cannot be said that a 'sound' person, who sees the things of life as they are, must have hope or else something is wrong—this can *not* be said if hope is understood expressly and in principle in purely *intra*-mundane terms. For 'sound', perspicacious sense does not *necessarily* respond correctly by hoping, to that which exists or may be expected to occur in the world. Hope as a human attitude which is correct, sound, true 'anyhow' and 'of itself' and 'in any case', only exists as hope of a salvation whose ground is not intra-mundane. (In comparison with this, a proposition like the following, which concludes a recent treatise on *Christianity and Philosophy*:[1] 'Hope in a future beyond the grave has been transmuted into hope in the future in this life between the present and death', must seem to the Christian the expression of an utter lack of hope.)

This hope of Christians, however, although it is not founded on purely intra-mundane considerations, is not of such a kind that the man who hopes thus loses sight (or even, *must* lose sight) of visible, terrestrial created reality, of this world that stretches out before our eyes. Not only can 'that' eternal life be initially experienced, by the person who is blessed, already *within* 'this' historical existence. This created world itself is explicitly included in the supra-natural hope. If hope means that the hoping person says (no, lives), 'It will turn out all right, it will have a happy ending', we must ask, *what* will turn out all right, *what* will have a happy ending? Well, to begin with, the existence of the person hoping himself. But is it not simultaneously affirmed—since the goal-image of the Christian's hope bears the name 'New Heaven and New Earth'—that this mundane reality which meets concrete experience, this 'waiting' creation in its entirety, will also turn out all right and, beyond all expectation, have a 'happy ending'?

Therefore, despite the fact that the Christian's attitude to history includes preparation for a catastrophic end within history, it nevertheless contains as an inalienable element the affirmation of created reality. To create a vital link between these seeming irreconcilables is a task that challenges the courage of the most valiant hearts, precisely in times when the temptation to despair is strong. Thus it is a distinguishing mark of the Christian martyr that in him 'no word is raised against God's creation'. This, says Erik Peterson, who has formulated this wonderful insight in his interpretation of the Apocalypse[2] —this is something *which distinguishes* the Christian martyr: He does not *revile* natural mundane reality, he finds creation, in spite of everything, 'very good'; whereas it is characteristic of the gnostic, who shuns the blood-testimony, that he speaks ill of creation and of natural things.[3]

And the Antichrist too is hostile to creation. Against his demand for totality, it is by no means solely the 'sacred' and the 'supra-natural' which the *ecclesia martyrum* defends, but equally the 'natural' goods grounded in the created nature of man, for example his personal dignity and his freedom. (Seen from the body of experience afforded by our own epoch, is it so unlikely that the Church, although ultimately concerned with a salvation that cannot be grounded on intra-mundane considerations, might remain the sole champion of the natural dignity of man?)

The Christian attitude to history contains both affirmation of creation and readiness for the blood-testimony; only the man who combines in himself this affirmation and this readiness will retain the possibility of historical activity, arising out of a genuine inner impulse, even in the midst of the catastrophe.

In this structure there is mirrored, however, another fundamental form, which lies at a deeper level and lends its stamp to the innermost nature of every historical being, the fact that 'the merely logical element in humanity is excluded from the stages and gradations in which the divine plan accomplishes its incomprehensible, grand history' (Konrad Weiss in his essay *The Christian Epimetheus*,[4] which meditates upon the inscrutability of the enigma of history). It is the fundamental form which, in the veiled manifestness of the *mysterium*, as a quintessence of all history, has come to realization in the 'event of salvation *per se*', which brings creation to completion, although its visible shape within history was an ignominious downfall. And it is the mysterious, but at the same time very real share in this fundamental pattern of history which effects authentic deliverance and salvation even in the downfall of the witness to truth.

However, this truth is not accessible to the bare will to knowledge alone, no matter how earnest and cognizant the latter may be. Beyond this it requires 'initiation'. And again this domain should, perhaps, be subject to a kind of *disciplina arcani, which would then have simultaneously to incorporate the tenet of the catastrophic end of time within history.*

This is the place to recall the example of St. Thomas. In the year 1255, the two Generals of their respective orders, John of Parma of the Franciscans, and Humbert of Romans of the Dominicans, issued a joint encyclical concerning the Apocalyptic significance of the two mendicant orders, which, according to the prophecy of Joachim Fiore, 'the Lord has aroused at the end of terrestrial time': the two candles in the Church, the two cherubim of the Ark of the Covenant, the two witnesses of Christ clothed in sackcloth, the two stars of the sybil[5]—and so on. This may show how deeply imbued with Apocalyptic ideas and emotions those years must have been during which the thirty-year-old Dominican monk, Thomas Aquinas, was preparing, as a baccalaureus, to become a public teacher at the University of Paris. And yet in the work of Thomas himself hardly a breath of this emotion is to be perceived; the attention of this great teacher of created reality, for whom, none the less, preparedness for the world dominion of evil at the end of time,[6] as well as the strict duty of readiness for the blood-testimony,[7] were numbered amongst the self-evident components of a true doctrine of life— the attention of St. Thomas seems so completely drawn towards the plenitude of reality, and therefore of good, in the created order as well as in the *ordo gratiae*, that the atmosphere of his work is wholly derived from this point. Of course, this indication carries weight only in so far as it refers to St. Thomas not as the 'greatest systemizer of high scholasticism', but as the *doctor communis ecclesiae*.

Or—in the official utterances of the Church, there is little question of such eschatological aspects; they treat rather of the possibilities of creating order in the world by prophylactic and curative action.

And thus, in so far as the inner style of such important utterances can be regarded as providing a firm criterion, the Christian attitude to history would appear to be characterized less by perpetual contemplation of the final catastrophe, than by a mute readiness, and most of all by activity within history, which is, of course, not deaf to the information given by the prophecy of the End, but which adheres soberly to the concrete tasks before it. However, the crucial as well as distinctive factor remains that the mastery of these same tasks is felt to be meaningful from the point of view of that same hope which also renders the blood-testimony intelligible and acceptable as a form of salvation.

Now, if the present situation is characterized by the fact that even the purely immanent, 'culture-sociological' conception of history is disposed to envisage the possibility of a catastrophic end as to be expected or even imminent, a special conclusion arises for him who is meditating upon history as a whole. At the beginning of this discussion I stated that it is impossible to philosophize unless one returns to a traditional fund of truth believed to have been revealed, and that this applies 'above all' to philosophizing about history. Above and beyond this, the following conclusion is inescapable: Without a return to revealed truth it is impossible not only to *philosophize* about history, but even to *live* in the area of real history as a spiritual being: that is to say, as a being who looks with open eyes upon what really happens in the real world, omitting nothing and glossing over nothing, but also abandoning and retracting nothing of that upon which man, by his very nature, cannot cease to set his hopes.

Finis

NOTES

The first prefatory quotation is to be found in Hamann's *Kreuzzüge des Philologen*, in the piece entitled *Kleeblatt hellenistischer Briefe*. *Hamanns Schriften*, publ. Friedrich Roth (Berlin, 1821-43) ii, 217.

The second quotation comes from a posthumous essay by Konrad Weiss, entitled *Logos des Bildes*.

CHAPTER I

1 *Meteorologica*, i, 3.

2 M. Heidegger, *Vom Wesen der Wahrheit* (Frankfort, 1943), p. 13.

3 Ibid., p. 13.

4 Fedor Stepun reports (in his memoirs *Vergangenes und Unvergängliches*, Munich, 1947, Bd. I, 122 f.) an experience from the philosophical seminary of Wilhelm Windelband, which is very characteristic in this respect.

5 Plato, *Phaidon*, 98.

6 *Summa theologica*, i, 106, 4 ad 3.

7 Fritz Kaufmann, *Geschichtsphilosophie der Gegenwart* (Berlin, 1931).

8 As regards Heidegger's category of 'historicity', this is certainly a philosophic category in the strict

sense; it is not a category of philosophy of history, however, but a category of philosophic anthropology.

10 The expression likewise originates from Alfred Weber. '*Der vierte Mensch oder der Zusammenbruch der geschichtlichen Kultur*'. *Die Wandlung*, 3 *Jg.* (1948), p. 287.

11 *Philebos*, 16.

12 In this connexion it must be noted that theology in this sense is scarcely possible without a genuinely philosophical attitude (and to some extent also, without philosophical training). This does not imply primarily that particular philosophic concepts and terms (e.g. substance-accident) are necessary to the pronouncement of a particular content of revelation (e.g. the doctrine of transubstantiation). What is meant is that the import of the pronouncement of revelation as a whole becomes intelligible to the interpreter—i.e. the theologian—in the act of spiritual appropriation, only if his gaze is already focused upon, and prepared for, the dimension 'roots of things', 'ultimate reality'.

13 Pascal, *Pensées*, Article VI, 38.

14 Matthew 11, 6.

15 *Grammar of Assent* (1870), Longmans, Green and Co. (London, 1930), p. 446.

16 Philipp Dessauer, *Das bionome Geschichtsbild* (Freiburg, 1946), p. 38.

17 *Grammar of Assent*, p. 446.

18 Philipp Dessauer, *Das bionome Geschichtsbild*, p. 45.

19 Commentary on the *Liber de causis,* 2, 6.

20 See Josef Pieper, *Wahrheit der Dinge* (Munich, 1948).

21 Werner Jaeger, *Aristoteles* (Berlin, 1923), p. 404.

22 Hans Leisegang, '*Über die Behandlung des scholastischen Satzes Quodlibet ens est unum, verum, bonum seu perfectum und seine Bedeutung in Kants Kritik der reinen Vernunft.' Kantstudien,* 20 Jg. (1915), p. 421.

CHAPTER II

1 *Wille zur Macht,* 3.

2 Ibid., 24.

3 Thomas Aquinas, *Summa theologica,* iii, 13, 2.

4 *Quaestiones disputatae de Potentia Dei,* 5, 3 ad 14.

5 Ibid., 5, 4 ad 6; Commentary on the *Liber Sententiarum,* 4, 46, 1, 3 ad 6; 2, 2, 1 ad 4.

6 Thomas Aquinas, *Summa theologica,* iii, 13, 2.

7 Ibid., i, 104, 3 ad 3.

8 Thomas Aquinas, *Quaestiones quodlibetales,* 4, 4.

9 Thomas Aquinas, Commentary on the *Liber Sententiarum,* 1, 8, 3, 2.

10 ThomasAquinas, *Summa theologica,* i, 65, 1 ad 1.

11 Thomas Aquinas, *Quaestiones disputatae de Potentia Dei,* 5, 9 ad 1.

12 2, 30. See also *Summa theologica,* i, 75, 6 ad 2.

13 Ibid., i, 104, 1 ad 4.

14 Ibid.

15 11, 14.

16 *Compendium theologica*, 1, 8.

17 Thus a poem by Armand Robin (quoted in the *Merkur* 1. *Jg.* (1947), p. 789) entitled *Le programme en quelques siècles.*

18 *Gesammelte Briefe* (Insel edition), Ernst Bertram, p. 88.

19 pp. 241 f.

20 *Progress and Religion* (London, Sheed and Ward, 1937), p. 228.

21 German translation by E. Müller-Kamp (Bonn, 1947), pp. 130, 200.

22 *The Era of Atomic Power* (Student Christian Movement Press, London, 1946), p. 59.

23 *Der vierte Mensch*, etc., p. 283.

24 *Atomenergie und Atombombe* (Frankfort, 1948), p. 294.

25 22, 30.

26 See in this connexion Herbert Grundmann, *Studien über Joachim von Floris* (Leipzig, 1927), pp. 92 ff.

27 In the *Zusätze über Ursprung und Beschaffenheit der heutigen Krisis* added to his famous essay *Die geschlichtlichen Krisen. Weltgeschichtliche Betrachtungen* (Kröner's pocket edition), pp. 204 f.

28 *Ideen zur Philosophie der Geschichte der Menschheit*, 9, 5.

29 Franz Borkenau, *Hundert Jahre Marxismus.* Merkur 2. Jg. (1948).

30 See W. Windelband, *Präludien* (Tübingen, 1924), i, p. 268.

31 *Ideen zur Philosophie der Geschichte*, 15, 4 (chapter heading).

32 Dawson, *Progress and Religion*, p. 201.

33 *Anti-Dühring*, trans. Emile Burns (Martin Lawrence, London), pp. 328–9.

34 Quoted in the periodical *Aufbau 2. Jg.* (1946), p. 890.

35 Eckart von Sydow, *Der Gedanke des Idealreichs in der idealistischen Philosophie von Kant bis Hegel* (Leipzig, 1914), p. 1.

36 Speech at the reception of the high-school workers in the Kremlin (17th May, 1938), reprinted in Lenin, *Ausgewählte Werke* (Moscow, 1946), *Bd. I*, 52.

37 In a footnote to the title.

38 Fifth sentence.

39 Eighth sentence.

40 Sixth sentence.

41 Eighth sentence.

42 Ninth sentence.

43 In the concluding note.

44 In Prussia permission to print this treatise, which was originally to have appeared in the *Berlinische Monatschrift*, was refused, whereupon permission was given by the Faculty of Philosophy in Jena. It was later included by Kant in the larger book *Die Religion innerhalb der Grenzen der blossen Vernunft*, as the third piece.

45 Part One, Section VII (heading).

46 Ibid., towards the end.

47 Ibid.

48 This treatise was also not allowed to appear in Berlin; permission to print was then obtained in Halle. Kant first published the treatise in 1798 in the book *Der Streit der Fakultäten* and, oddly enough, (as Section Two) under the title *Der Streit der philosophischen Fakultät mit der juristischen.*

49 Section Three.

50 *The Era of Atomic Power*, p. 20.

51 Section Five.

52 Because, as is stated a little earlier, the utterance of this 'sympathy' 'was itself fraught with danger'.

53 Section Six.

54 To Johann von Müller, 1789.

55 Section Seven.

56 Section One, note.

57 Section One.

58 Ibid.

59 Section Two.

60 Section Three.

61 *Ob das menschliche Geschlecht im beständigen Fortschreiten zum Besseren sei*, 2. *Abschnitt.*

62 It is perhaps permissible to report here a personal experience. In a collection of *sententiae* from the works of St. Thomas Aquinas, *The Human Wisdom of St. Thomas*, Sheed and Ward, London and New York, 1948, I also quoted some sentences relating to the Antichrist. These texts, and *exclusively* these, were described in a theological journal as 'pieces of less value'.

63 *The Era of Atomic Power*, p. 44.

64 *Idee zu einer allgemeinen Geschichte in welt-bürgerlicher Absicht*, ninth sentence.

65 Published by Fritz Medicus (*Philosophische Bibliothek*), Leipzig, p. 12.

66 Ibid., p. 12.

67 Ibid., pp. 12 f.

68 Ibid., p. 13.

69 Ibid., p. 14.

70 Ibid., p. 16.

71 Ibid., p. 17.

72 *Der Sieg des Guten Prinzips*, etc., Part Two.

73 *Grundzüge des Gegenwärtigen Zeitalters*, p. 24.

74 Ibid., p. 103.

75 First address.

76 H. von Campenhausen, *Weltgeschichte und Gottesgericht* (Stuttgart, 1947), p. 11.

77 J. von Görres, *Über die Grundlage, Gliederung und Zeitenfolge der Weltgeschichte*. Three lectures (Breslau, 1830), p. 113.

78 Ibid.

79 Ibid., pp. 110 f.

80 J. Thyssen, *Geschichte der Geschichtsphilosophie* (Berlin, 1936), p. 88.

81 See Paul Menzer, *Kants Lehre von der Entwicklung in Natur und Geschichte* (Berlin, 1911), p. 253.

82 L. Emrich, *Europa 1975* (Freiburg, 1946), pp. 24 f.

83 Menzer, *Kants Lehre von der Entwicklung*, p. 203.

84 *Idee zu einer allgemeinen Geschichte*, sixth sentence.

85 E. R. Curtius, *Toynbees Geschichtslehre. Merkur* 2. *Jg.*, p. 509.

86 Bertrand Russell, quoted in R. Niebuhr, *Jenseits der Tragödie* (Munich, 1947), p. 66.

CHAPTER III

1 See Hans Preuss, *Die Vorstellungen vom Antichrist im späteren Mittelalter, bei Luther und in der konfessionellen Polemik* (Leipzig, 1906), p. 27.

2 See ibid., p. 265.

3 J. Döllinger, *Christentum und Kirche in der Zeit der Grundlegung* (Regensburg, 1860), p. 431.

4 Preuss, *Die Vorstellungen vom Antichrist*, p. 257.

5 Ibid., p. 448.

6 Ibid., p. 21.

7 Defence speech.

8 Raïssa Maritain, *Der Fürst dieser Welt. Der katholische Gedanke* 7. *Jg.* (1934), pp. 88–93.

9 *Der Christ und die Geschichte* (Leipzig, 1935), p. 124.

10 Ibid., p. 92.

11 It is not clear whether this statement (*Merkur*, 2. *Jg.*, 1948) is to be understood as reproducing Toynbee's opinion.

12 *Noten und Abhandlungen zu besserem, Verständnis des West-Östlichen Divans.* Chapter: *Israel in der Wüste.*

13 *Zeuge der Wahrheit* (Leipzig, 1937), p. 91.

14 Commentary on II Epistle to the Thessalonians chap. 2. lect. 2.

15 Ibid., lect. 1.

16 *Strahlungen* (Tübingen, 1949), p. 469.

17 *Era of Atomic Power*, p. 44.

18 G. Nebel, *Bei den nördlichen Hesperiden* (Wuppertal, 1948), p.258.

19 *Ausgewählte Werke* (Moscow, 1946), *Bd. II*, p. 236.

20 Letter of 16.6.88.

21 Herman Rauschning, *Die Zeit des Deliriums*, extracts quoted in *Die Welt* (Hamburg), of 4.12.1949.

22 Peter de Mendelssohn in *Der Monat*, 2. *Jg.* (1949), p. 162.

23 *Zeuge der Wahrheit*, pp. 81 ff.

24 Ibid., p. 82.

25 Ibid.

26 Ethelbert Stauffer, *Theologie des Neuen Testaments*, 3rd edition, pp. 192 ff.

27 A. Huxley speaks (*Gedanken über des Fortschritt. Neue Schweizer Rundschau. Jg.*, 1948) of a 'gigantic eugenic experiment', which could hardly be carried out 'without the pressure of a world dictatorship'; at the same time he says: 'It would be an appropriate punishment for the presumptuous *hubris* of man, if' —since most mutations are harmful —'the final result were to culminate in the breeding of a race of hare-lipped, six-fingered idiots.' P. 400.

28 Thus E. R. Curtius in his Toynbee essay. *Merkur* 2. *Jg.* (1948), p. 505.

29 Philipp Dessauer, *Das bionome Geschichtsbild*, p. 40.

30 H. Schlier, *Vom Antichrist. Theologische Aufsätze zum* 50. *Geburtstag von Karl Barth.* Publ. Ernst Wolf (Munich, 1936), p. 115.

31 Thomas Aquinas: *dicens se Deum et hominem.* Commentary on II Epistle to the Thessalonians, chap. 2, lect. 2.

32 Schlier, *Antichrist*, p. 121.

33 Stauffer, *Theologie des Neuen Testaments*, p. 194.

34 Peterson, *Zeuge der Wahrheit*, p. 83.

35 Hans Preuss, *Der Antichrist*, 2nd edition 1909, p. 41.

36 The fact has been remarked upon that in the Greek of St. Mark's Gospel the word 'abomination', quoted from Daniel (9, 27; 12, 11), which is neuter, is used, contrary to every grammatical rule, as masculine and thus gives the idea of a male person.

37 Commentary on II Epistle to the Thessalonians, chap. 2, lect. 1.

38 K. Thieme, *Am Ziel der Zeiten?* (Salzburg-Leipzig, 1939), p. 30.

39 *Rheinischer Merkur* (Coblenz) of 19.2.1949.

40 E. Peterson, *Die Kirche aus Juden und Heiden* (Salzburg, 1933), p. 71.

41 II Thessalonians, 2, 7.

42 For example Erik Peterson, who speaks of the possiblity (*Kirche aus Juden und Heiden*, p. 59) that

'the end of the world will be held up by the unbelief of Israel.'

43 See Preuss, *Die Vorstellungen vom Antichrist*, pp. 18 ff.

44 *Drei Gespräche*, p. 181.

45 In a scholarly work on the eschatology of the Eastern Church, which appeared in Germany between 1933 and 1945, this particular feature in the conception of the Antichrist, his vegetarianism, was for obvious reasons suppressed (Hitler, too, was a vegetarian!).

46 Dionysius of Luxemburg, a literary forerunner of P. Martin of Cochem. See Preuss, *Die Vorstellungen vom Antichrist*, p. 254.

47 *Drei Gespräche*, p. 200.

48 Thus E. Stauffer, *Theologie des Neuen Testaments*, p. 192. Schlier (*Vom Antichrist*, p. 119): 'In the beast the historical cosmos finds its unity.'

49 *Elend der Philosophie. Historischer Materialismus* (Kröner's pocket edition), ii, 574.

50 *Der Vierte Mensch*, p. 290.

51 Stauffer, *Theologie des Neuen Testaments*, p. 194.

52 A. Wikenhauser in his commentary on the Apocalypse (*Regensburger Neues Testament*), Regensburg, 1947, p. 90.

53 Schlier, *Vom Antichrist*, p. 121.

54 Jung-Stilling, *Erster Nachtrag zur Siegesgeschichte der christlichen Religion* (1805) (quoted in Schlier, *Vom Antichrist*, p. 119, note 11).

55 Schlier, *Vom Antichrist*, p. 122.

56 *Ende aller Dinge*, concluding sentence.

57 Stauffer, *Theologie des Neuens Testaments*, pp. 192 ff.

58 Commentary on II Epistle to the Thessalonians, chap. 2, lect. 2.

CONCLUSION

1 Walter Bröcker in *Studium Generale* 1. *Jg.* (1948), p. 214.

2 *Zeuge der Wahrheit*, p. 52.

3 Ibid., p. 91.

4 Berlin, 1933, pp. 33 f.

5 A. Dempf, *Sacrum Imperium* (Munich-Berlin 1929), p. 303.

6 See for instance the oft-quoted commentary on II Epistle to the Thessalonians.

7 *Quaestiones quodlibetales*, 4, 20.

INDEX